T0330789

TEACHING LAW AND CRIMINAL JUSTICE THROUGH POPULAR CULTURE

A Deep Learning Approach
in the Streaming Era

TEACHING LAW AND CRIMINAL JUSTICE THROUGH POPULAR CULTURE

A Deep Learning Approach
in the Streaming Era

Julian Hermida, DCL

First edition published 2022

Apple Academic Press Inc.
1265 Goldenrod Circle, NE,
Palm Bay, FL 32905 USA

4164 Lakeshore Road, Burlington,
ON, L7L 1A4 Canada

CRC Press
6000 Broken Sound Parkway NW,
Suite 300, Boca Raton, FL 33487-2742 USA

2 Park Square, Milton Park,
Abingdon, Oxon, OX14 4RN UK

© 2022 Apple Academic Press, Inc.

Apple Academic Press exclusively co-publishes with CRC Press, an imprint of Taylor & Francis Group, LLC

Library and Archives Canada Cataloguing in Publication

Title: Teaching law and criminal justice through popular culture : a deep learning approach in the streaming era / Julian Hermida, PhD.

Names: Hermida, Julian, author.

Description: First edition. | Includes bibliographical references and index.

Identifiers: Canadiana (print) 20210102004 | Canadiana (ebook) 20210102012 | ISBN 9781771889414 (hardcover) | ISBN 9781003084204 (ebook)

Subjects: LCSH: Law—Study and teaching (Higher) | LCSH: Criminal justice, Administration of—Study and teaching (Higher) | LCSH: Popular culture in education. | LCSH: Learning. | LCSH: College teaching.

Classification: LCC K100 .H47 2021 | DDC 340.07—dc23

Library of Congress Cataloging-in-Publication Data

....

CIP data on file with US Library of Congress

....

ISBN: 978-1-77188-941-4 (hbk)
ISBN: 978-1-77463-793-7 (pbk)
ISBN: 978-1-00308-420-4 (ebk)

About the Author

Julian Hermida is Associate Professor at Algoma University's Department of Law (Sault Ste. Marie, Ontario, Canada). He was also the Chair of Algoma University's Teaching and Learning Committee for several years. Julian has a very successful practice of more than 15 years of full-time teaching at all levels. Prior to joining Algoma, he taught at Dalhousie University (Halifax, NS, Canada), where he was recognized with the Award for Excellence for Teaching and Learning.

A seasoned educational developer, Julian has ample experience designing, implementing, and evaluating university-wide faculty development programs and initiatives. He has conducted educational development workshops and led seminars on teaching and learning in Canada, the United States, Europe, and Latin America. He has won several grants to fund his scholarship of teaching and learning research projects on deep learning.

Julian Hermida holds master's and doctoral degrees from McGill University's Faculty of Law. He did his postdoctoral studies at the University of Ottawa. He has also received formal education and training in higher education teaching in a unique and intensive program offered at the University of Montreal as well as in educational development programs in Canada and the United States. These include the Best Teachers Institute led by Ken Bain and Alverno College Assessment workshop, among others.

Julian has published extensively on a wide array of both teaching and learning and legal topics. He has more than 100 publications, including his book *Facilitating Deep Learning: Pathways to Success for University and College Teachers*, published by Apple Academic Press.

Prior to working full time in academia, Julian Hermida practiced law in New York, Montreal, and Buenos Aires.

Contents

Acknowledgments

This book is the result of years of teaching to create a deep learning environment through popular culture stories. It is also the result of meaningful conversations, conference participations, and multiple research projects.

First and foremost, I would like to thank and dedicate this book to my wife and "partner in crime" for the invaluable conversations and challenging exchanges of ideas on teaching and learning, motivation, and research methods. This book would not have been possible without our shared—popular culture—stories. A deep and heartfelt thank you goes to Laura!

I am also indebted to my students, particularly those who took the class discussed in Chapter 8, most of whom are now successful professionals who use the competences advocated in the book.

I would also like to acknowledge a research grant given by the University of Flores to write part of this book, especially Chapter 8.

I am equally grateful to my colleagues who participate in the faculty development initiatives that I regularly lead.

Through his conferences, publications, conversations, and his Best Teachers Institute, Ken Bain has profoundly transformed the way I think about teaching. Multiple references to his work throughout the book are evidence of the great influence he has had in my teaching and educational development practice.

My thanks also go to my publishers at Apple Academic Press, Ashish Kumar, Rakesh Kumar, and Sandra Sickels, for their confidence and encouragement in writing another book for AAP as well as for their patience in waiting for me to finish the manuscript.

Disclaimer

References to films, TV shows, and books are made under the fair use/fair dealing doctrine and are made with the purpose of research and education. They are not meant to decrease their value. On the contrary, it is expected that these references will act as a catalyst to further viewing and reading the works referenced throughout this book.

PART 1

Deep Learning

CHAPTER 1

Introduction

> The news is the first rough draft of history.
>
> The Post (Spielberg, 2017)

ABSTRACT

Deep learning is a committed approach to learning where learners learn for life and can apply what they learn to new situations and contexts. Deep learning involves discovering and constructing knowledge by negotiating meanings with peers and by making connections between existing and new knowledge. According to many scholarly studies reported in the literature, most higher education students approach learning in a surface way, soon forget what they learn, and cannot use it meaningfully outside the classroom. Popular culture enhances the deep learning process by helping students develop cognitive skills, competences, and practices that are essential for the professional practice of law and criminal justice and that are often neglected in traditional law school and criminal justice curricula. These include rapid cognition and other similar thought processes, metacognition, the interpretation and production of popular culture texts, the narration of stories, and effective communication with the press, among others.

1.1 INTRODUCTION

I grew up watching films and TV shows and, yes, I continue binging on series and movies streaming online. I had a well-rounded childhood, but films and TV shows occupied a very special room in my heart. As a teenager, I was part of a film group. We made shorts and documentaries. I wrote scripts, edited, and even directed. I also acted as executive producer.

And I was involved in promoting and marketing our films. I wrote dozens, if not hundreds, of press releases. I talked to the press on many occasions. I participated in film festivals around the world and also organized a handful of film festivals myself. Whereas I loved the film industry, I always knew I wanted to be a lawyer. I dreamed of litigating in a criminal court much like the lawyers I loved to watch on TV and the big screen. I wanted to go the extra mile to find out the real perpetrator of the crime to help my client. I knew it would be exciting to pull off a last minute trick to save an innocent defendant. I dreamed of building a reputation as a bold criminal lawyer.

My first experience in a law firm after I had finished law school was nothing like my dreams. The very first assignment, and my first disappointment with the legal education I had received, had to do with a contract. It was a large, general practice law firm with hundreds of lawyers, serving mainly corporate clients in virtually all branches of law, including criminal law. One of the senior partners asked me to come to his office. I had thought he would take me to the courtroom to shadow him while he cross-examined a police officer or he would ask me to help him prepare the opening statement of a multimillion dollar fraud case. He told me I had to read a draft of a contract written by the other party's counsel and suggest changes to improve our client's position. He gave me a file with a few documents that did not explain much. That was it. Although I would have preferred to be involved in a criminal case, since it was my first assignment I worked hard and enthusiastically. I looked for examples in other files. I checked some books. I looked at some model contracts. I suggested changes to the language of a few clauses. I even proposed some new provisions. I spotted some mistakes, such as references to inexistent appendices, grammar errors, and page numbers. Given the lack of support and the limited directions, I thought I had done a good job. At the end of the day, I gave my comments to the draft to the senior partner. He was busy and did not have time to look at it then. The following morning, he told me that he had forwarded the contract to the client and the other party's law firm for its execution. Later that same day, the senior partner summoned me to his office. The tone of his voice predicted trouble. He told me that I had forgotten to include a clause in the contract stating that the other party would have to assume all taxes. He added that this mistake had cost our client a lot of money. He admitted that it was partially his fault too, because he did not carefully check what I had done, as he had been very busy with other issues. I was very upset with myself. Apart from contracts—a required course—I had taken advanced courses in contracts, tax law, and business law at law school. I must admit that in all these courses I had seen that this was an expected clause. I had even taken an ethics course where I had read a case about a lawyer who had neglected to negotiate this clause. An essay involving this issue appeared in a final exam. I had aced all these courses. I blamed my education for making me learn in a way that I soon forgot and for not teaching me how to apply what I learned to a real context.

After that episode, the senior partner kept me in the sidelines and assigned me low-level work such as looking for precedents, proofreading memos, making photocopies, filing documents, and even typing things up. I knew my dreams of litigating a criminal case would have to wait.

One Friday evening a few weeks after this incident, everyone at the law firm seemed to be swamped with work. There were several initial public offerings going on at the same time, together with the negotiation of some major contracts, the merger of some giant international corporations, and the defense of a CEO charged with insider trading. It must have been around 8 p.m. when the same senior partner called me to his office. I feared he would give some bad news connected to the contract incident. But, to my surprise, he assigned me substantial work again. A major client had asked our firm to file an injunction against its competition for a comparative advertising campaign, which, according to the senior partner, seemed 100% legal. He asked me to see what I could come up with, but he insisted that the law was clear about the legality of an advertising campaign that surveyed consumers about preferences between two products. He said it would be OK if I concluded that we could not do anything. In that case, he would call the client on Monday and advise against filing the injunction.

I quickly reviewed the law applicable to comparative advertising. There was no doubt that comparing consumer preference in advertising was legal, provided that the company conducting the campaign had supporting evidence of its claims and that it duly acknowledged the ownership of its competition's trademark. I had a look at the file which the senior partner had given me, which contained copies of the legal disclaimers shown at the end of the advertisement. There was evidence that the competition recognized our client's trademark. Most important, the file clearly indicated the existence of evidence supporting the survey. Our client's competition had conducted blind taste tests between the two products. At supermarkets, at shopping malls, and at the intersection of high-traffic streets, consumers were asked to taste both products without knowing which products they were tasking and to choose their preferred one. After that, the preferred product was revealed. In most cases, consumers expressed preference for our client's competition's product. These tests were filmed and shown in a series of short commercials on national television.

Later that evening, the senior partner called me and asked me if I agreed with his preliminary observation. I told him that I had just finished reading everything and that I had the same opinion as he did from reading the file, but I needed a few more hours to give him a definitive opinion. He said it was OK. He would come the following morning to prepare for an opening statement in a criminal case, and we could meet in his office to discuss this issue. But he insisted that there would not be much that we could do.

I had a hunch. I did not tell him I did because it would not sound professional. But I had watched some of the commercials on TV at home that week. So, I called our client and asked for a tape of the commercials, which I got almost immediately. I took the tape home, and after a very late dinner, I watched the commercials. My instinct told me that there was something fishy. I did not know what it was, but I felt there was something wrong. I knew that literally millions of viewers had watched the commercials on TV, including our client's advertising agency, which according to the information on the file, had analyzed the commercials from an advertising perspective and had found no problems at all. I decided to play the tapes frame by frame. Low and behold, I realized that our client's competition had used its own products for the blind taste tests and had not included our client's product. So, in most cases, consumers were asked to taste the same product twice without ever tasting our client's product. It was no wonder they would not choose our client's product. I was elated. I had found out something that no one had seen before. I knew instantly that this would be a homerun in court. I wrote a short memo with my findings. Although it was very late and I was tired, I tossed and turned in bed without falling asleep. I was anxious to tell my senior partner what I had found out the following morning. I finally fell asleep at around 5 a.m. and woke up at 7 a.m. The first thing I did was to read my memo and watch the commercials again frame by frame. I feared that I had hallucinated this or that the findings were part of a dream. Relieved, I confirmed that what I had discovered about the commercials was real.

When I met the senior partner in his office that morning, he was surprised. He called our client. Their first reaction was that of disbelief. I had to show our client's general counsel the tape frame by frame. He brought in top executives from the advertising agency, who confirmed my findings. On Monday, the senior partner and I filed an injunction against our client's competition. We obtained the injunction and stopped the campaign. I was excited. I was the hero of the day. I soon became famous in my law firm, and every senior partner wanted to work with me. Our client was as happy as grateful. The CEO came to our office and gave me a gold watch as a present—a gesture that it is not very common in large law firms serving corporate clients.

However, our client's competition launched a fierce press campaign. They contacted the most prominent journalists. They held press conferences. They issued press releases. They sent a very clear message to the general public and the judges. They had made a mistake in the editing of the TV commercials, but they assured that they had asked consumers to compare both products and not just theirs. I begged the senior partner to talk to the press and counterattack our client's competition's claims. But the senior partner, a very traditional, conservative, and even fearful person, was against dealing with the press. He repeated over and over that lawyers speak in court and not on television. Our client's competition appealed the injunction. They argued the editors had made a mistake. The court of appeals sided with them and lifted the injunction.

I felt frustrated and hated the senior partner for his cowardliness, dearth of vision, and above all, for his lack of support. This episode, together with the contract incident, would have a profound impact on my professional career. I had decided to quit the practice of law as soon as I could and devote to teaching law. Although I had to continue practicing law for a few years until I had the money to go back to graduate school, I knew my days as a practicing attorney were numbered.

I wanted to learn how legal education needed to change and improve to better prepare graduates for all aspects of an increasingly complex professional practice.

1.2 DEEP LEARNING AND SURFACE LEARNING

My law school years did not prepare me to remember what I learned at school or to apply what I learned in new contexts and new cases. My education had consisted of listening to professors talking about law, answering their questions, and reading about law. Although I had a couple of clinical courses, those courses had not helped me either with the intricacies of legal practice.

I felt that my years as an amateur filmmaker and my passion for popular culture shows prepared me better for legal practice than law school. I developed a host of cognitive skills that proved very useful throughout my career, but which were not part of my law school education. I had learned to follow my instincts, to make intuitive decisions, to think of the subtext of any human interaction, to make connections to other texts and situations, to solve problems, to deconstruct hidden aspects of a story, to challenge authority, and to judge the quality of work. I had also developed other skills that helped me win many cases that were not part of my formal education, either. I had learned how to talk to the press and win their support. I had learned how to narrate stories and how to use audiovisual materials to tell these stories.

As from my early days of legal practice, I wanted to know why I had forgotten about something I had studied several times at law school. How was it possible that I had no idea about something that I had learned not that long ago? Would I teach my students in the same way? Would they forget everything after taking my courses? If so, why? Is there something structurally wrong in higher education that prevents students from learning in a way that they will remember? Or was I alone in having done something wrong that caused me to forget? How could I teach so that my students would learn for life? What could I do so that students could transfer and apply what they learn to other situations and contexts?

At the core of these questions lie two fundamental concepts, which I ignored at that time: deep learning and surface learning. Deep learning is a committed approach to learning where learners learn for life and can apply what they learn to new situations and contexts. Surface learning is a superficial approach to learning where students use knowledge that they acquire for writing exams or papers and soon forget it. Deep learners discover and construct their own knowledge by negotiating meanings with peers and by making connections between existing and new knowledge. Surface learners receive knowledge passively from their teachers or books.

One of the most shocking research findings about deep and surface learning reported in the literature in virtually every country and region in the Western world is that most higher education students approach learning in a surface way (Biggs and Tang, 2007). In other words, students forget what they learn and cannot use it meaningfully outside their classrooms.

In any other activity, industry, or sector, this would make headlines all over the world. For example, if car manufacturers produced cars that ran for a few miles only, if planes flew only a few minutes after take-off, or if computers stopped working after a few mouse clicks, it could not be business as usual in those industries. People would be fired, companies would be closed down, consumers would file multimillion dollar lawsuits, and society would demand immediate changes. Fortunately, higher education is different. We have time to work on our mistakes and fix them. We have time to go back to the drawing board and teach our courses differently. But unfortunately, it takes us too long to realize that things are not working well and even longer to find a meaningful solution. In the meantime, entire cohorts of students are sent out to the world outside academia having learned only superficially.

Deep learning is the answer to the performance problems in law school and criminal justice programs. It is what helps students become active protagonists of their own learning process. It is the key to their success in their future professional endeavors. It enables learners to connect, apply, and transfer knowledge to a wide array of settings and to act effectively in different contexts. Popular culture plays a key role in the deep learning process. When law and criminal justice are taught through popular culture within a deep learning environment, that is to say, when students learn to reflect about law and criminal justice through popular culture stories and when students learn to be effective interpreters and producers of popular culture texts, popular culture helps foster most of the intellectual skills and the professional competences needed to succeed in the legal and criminal justice fields, including those usually marginalized in higher education.

1.3 PURPOSE OF THE BOOK

This book aims to show what we can do to create a learning environment that encourages students to take a deep approach to learning through the use of popular culture stories in the law school and criminal justice classrooms. Popular culture enhances the deep learning process by helping students develop cognitive skills, competences, and practices that are essential for the professional practice of law and criminal justice and that are often neglected in traditional law school and criminal justice curricula. These skills include rapid cognition and other similar thought processes, metacognition, the interpretation and production of popular culture texts, the narration of stories, and effective communication with the press, among others.

By deconstructing the notion of deep learning and by examining the power of popular culture in law school and criminal justice programs, I will show you how to bring about deep learning in our law and criminal justice teaching practice. After reading this book, you will have the theoretically grounded and research-supported strategies and tools that are necessary to implement a deep learning environment through popular culture stories in law and criminal justice classes. Committing to fostering a deep learning environment in our classes is an urgent imperative. We owe it to our students.

1.4 CHARACTER ANALYSIS APPROACH

The analysis of the plays, films, TV shows, and their characters throughout the book follows a Stanislavskian theory of scene analysis (Stanislavski, 1936). The description of the selected scenes used to illustrate the main aspects of teaching for deep learning through popular culture is based on the analysis of the characters' back stories, objectives, beliefs, the subtext, the given circumstances, and the characters' reaction to the given circumstances. Thus, this description may include actions which the TV show, film, or play does not explicitly show but which one can assume based on a careful Stanislavskian scene and character analysis.

You can understand and engage with this book perfectly well whether or not you are familiar with the stories (films, TV shows, books, and songs) used for the discussion and explanation of the deep learning process and the role of popular culture. Needless to say, you do not need to choose the same works to implement a course on law—or criminal justice—and popular culture. Any relevant popular culture work will help enrich the deep learning process, if you include all the elements, strategies, and practices discussed throughout the book. On a related note, the main tenet of this book, i.e., that popular culture can enhance the learning process, applies to all disciplines and is not restricted to the law school and criminal justice classrooms.

Throughout the book I use popular culture stories for two different purposes. One obvious purpose is to give examples of how popular culture works can be incorporated into the classroom. The other purpose is to illustrate teaching and learning concepts such as deep and surface learning, metacognition, or rapid cognition.

Another important caveat: I do not claim that you can only create a deep learning environment if you teach through popular culture (Bain, 2004). What I do claim throughout the book is that popular culture stories can greatly enhance this process in the law and criminal justice disciplines.

1.5 ORGANIZATION OF THE BOOK

This book is divided into eight chapters. Chapter 1 contains this introduction, which situates the book in its context and states its main purpose. In Chapter 2, I will explore the reasons why students learn superficially by focusing on the signature pedagogies of law school and—graduate and undergraduate—criminal justice programs, that is to say, the way we teach. I will also address the notion of deep learning. I will delve into a detailed examination of the elements and factors of deep learning. Deep learning requires a series of cognitive and metacognitive interventions at both the individual and the group (social) levels so that learners can construct new knowledge that results in both a conceptual change in their cognitive structure and in their position in academic and professional communities[1]. In Chapter 3, I will explore a thought process (rapid cognition) that has traditionally been neglected in law schools and criminal justice programs, as well as in most other areas of higher education, despite its importance for professional practice.

Chapter 4 deals with motivation—a key factor in the deep learning process. I will analyze the types of motivation and their connection to learning. I will then examine the factors that foster intrinsic motivation

---

[1] I follow a constructivist approach to deep learning, as this approach is understood by Schwandt and McCarty (2000), who advanced the idea that "everyone who believes the mind is active in the making of knowledge is a constructivist" (Graffam, 2003). In this sense, constructivism is a point of departure, which includes doubts, debates, criticism, and self-criticism (Carretero, 2009). Constructivism is founded upon the idea that the individual is not a mere product of the social context or his or her internal dispositions, but rather his or her own construction that is produced every day as a result of the interaction between those two factors. At the same time, my conception of deep learning is compatible with vygotskian and neo-vygotskian notions of social learning and development. It is also compatible with findings in cognitive neuroscience (Zull, 2002). Cognitive neuroscience deals with research on brain processes and structures; it also examines the role that the brain plays in the learning process (Zull, 2011).

and the role that popular culture plays in the development of intrinsic motivation. In Chapter 5, I will analyze the stories embedded in academic disciplines. I will focus on the stories that law and criminal justice tell both inside and outside the courtroom. I will also compare the narrative structure of legal and criminal justice stories and stories told in popular culture. After briefly visiting the law and popular culture field, I will concentrate on the use of popular culture as primary sources for law and criminal justice teaching. Chapter 6 deals with media literacy. I will trace its evolution in educational settings and its current—marginal—role in law and criminal justice programs. I will discuss tools to help students both interpret and produce media texts connected to the practice of law and criminal justice. I will also explore ideas to design classroom activities to foster the development of media literacy in law school and criminal justice university courses. In Chapter 7, I will explore the notion of metacognition and how we can help students use metacognitive strategies to engage in reflection about their learning process and self-evaluation. The emphasis of this chapter will be on how we can use metacognitive categories to encourage students to take a deep approach in their learning process. Chapter 8 will recount an experience in planning and enacting a course on criminal law taught entirely through popular culture stories. The course aimed to help students examine criminal law deeply and to help them interpret and produce popular culture texts dealing with theoretical and practical issues of criminal law. Finally, the last chapter will offer a brief summary of the main ideas of this book, that is, that deep learning is the answer to the performance problem of law school and criminal justice programs and that the pathways, practices, tools, strategies, and initiatives developed in this book, which focus on the use of popular culture in our classes, can foster an environment that is conducive to deep learning.

KEYWORDS

- **deep learning**
- **teaching**
- **law**
- **criminal justice**
- **university**

CHAPTER 2

Teaching for Deep Learning

— Ma boum sans Mathieu, c'est même pas la peine.
— Mais non tout le monde y va, ça va être génial !
— J'm'en fous de tout le monde, c'est lui que je veux !

La Boum (Pinoteau, 1980)

ABSTRACT

The most influential factor in the quality of student learning is the way we teach. We can create the environment and conditions that can encourage our students to approach learning in a profound way. The signature pedagogies that predominate in the teaching of law and criminal justice, that is, the case-dialogue method, the lecture, and the seminar, with little or no emphasis in popular culture, do not contribute to the creation of deep learning environments. These pedagogies do not help students discover and construct knowledge by themselves and do not help students engage in the practices that members of the professional or academic communities routinely take part in. The deep learning process requires a connection between new knowledge, embedded in the input story in the form of a problem, question, or situation, and existing knowledge, which makes up our cognitive structure. This connection must activate a series of competences, skills, and processes both at the individual and social levels. Deep learning also requires constant reflection about the learning process and the changes at the individual (cognitive structure) and social levels (professional or academic community). Popular culture plays a very important role in the creation of a deep learning environment, as we all think in terms of stories. Furthermore, the deep learning process can be understood and processed as a story itself. This process contains several stories, mainly the input story, which is the central aspect of the process, and the existing stories, that are stored in the learners' mind.

2.1   INTRODUCTION

In the previous chapter, I discussed the notions of deep learning and surface learning. Succinctly, deep learning is learning for life, and surface learning is learning to complete a task in the short-term. Most law school and university students approach learning in a surface way (Biggs and Tang, 2007). In other words, students forget what they learn right after they pass their final examinations or write their final papers and cannot use it meaningfully outside the setting of higher education. The research literature shows that we teachers play the most influential role in students'—usually unconscious—decision to take a deep approach to learning. We can create the environment and conditions that can encourage our students to approach learning in a profound way.

I will begin the discussion in this chapter with an analysis of the main reasons why students learn superficially, that is to say, the way we teach at law schools and universities. I will focus on the signature pedagogies: the case-dialogue method (American law schools), the lecture (undergraduate criminal justice programs and law schools outside the United States), and the seminar (graduate criminal justice programs). Then, I will examine the notion of deep learning and compare it to the surface learning approach. I will also discuss the notion of popular culture and its connection to the deep learning process. Finally, I will break down and analyze every element of deep learning.

2.2   SURFACE LEARNING VS. DEEP LEARNING OR HORRIBLE HARRIET VS. THE LORD OF THE FLIES

In *Easter Egg Adventure* (Williams, 2004), directed by John Michael Williams, Ms. Horrible Harriet Hare has been teaching cohorts of Egg Town's students for decades. Virtually everyone in Egg Town has studied with her. Ms. Hare is very smart and has acute critical thinking skills. She enunciates very clearly and speaks with a very erudite vocabulary. Her voice sounds authoritative and reflects a vast knowledge of the disciplines she teaches. She seems to know the content well. Presumably, her colleagues regard her as a disciplinary expert. Her teaching focuses almost exclusively on lecturing students. Her lectures are impeccable. She gives lots of information to students. She explains the materials with precision and with plenty of details. She uses specific disciplinary vocabulary and corrects students when they do not use appropriate terminology. She expects students to absorb her explanations and to reproduce them with equal precision in traditional exams and papers. Students are not engaged in her class. They appear bored. Some are even afraid of her. Ms. Hare uses punishment (giving low grades, assigning extra work, even shaming students in front of others) to encourage her students to study and learn. Ms. Hare loves her work and honestly believes that she helps students learn by being strict and demanding. But most important for her, she believes in the power of her lectures. She thinks that the more erudite information she passes to her students, the more the students will learn.

In one of the first scenes, a mysterious takit (a big animal that seems to be a cross between an eagle and a rooster) covered in a red shawl, breaks into a bakery at night to steal money from the cash register. The owner, Boss Baker, wakes up and tries to stop the thief. He can hardly see the thief. He cannot even distinguish whether it is a male or a female takit, as it is very dark. Boss Baker manages to throw a pie at the thief before he escapes with the money. The pie leaves a stain on the thief's red shawl. The thief goes back home and returns the shawl to his mother, Tiny Tessie, who is sound asleep and does not know that her son, Terrible Timothy Takit, has just robbed the bakery.

The following morning, when Tiny Tessie, wearing her shawl, goes to the bakery to buy some plum cakes, the owner recognizes the stained shawl and accuses her of robbery. He calls the police. Meanwhile, neighbors and passersby gather outside the bakery. When Sargent O'Hare arrives, he interrogates Tiny Tessie. In front of the crowd that gathered to see what has happened, Sargent O'Hare asks her if she has robbed the bakery. Too ashamed for being accused of a crime she has not committed in front of her friends and acquaintances, Tiny Tessie remains quiet. Then, she breaks down and collapses. Her body shakes out of fear and embarrassment. The police and the onlookers take her silence and shaking as an admission of guilt. They think that this, together with the stained shawl she is wearing, is sufficient evidence of the crime. So, the police arrest Tiny Tessie for breaking and entering the bakery.

When Ms. Horrible Harriet Hare goes downtown and hears the people in Egg Town gossip about Tiny Tessie, she becomes furious, as she does not believe that Tiny Tessie has robbed the bakery. Ms. Hare argues vehemently with the people in Egg Town, all of whom are her former students, and—unsuccessfully—tries to persuade them that there is not sufficient evidence to prove that Tiny Tessie has robbed the bakery. Ms. Hare is frustrated because her former students cannot think critically. They have been easily convinced by the first explanation they hear about the case, even when this explanation does not hold water. They seem to have jumped into conclusions without fully examining every aspect of the situation. They have neglected to consider possible alternative explanations, and they cannot tell facts from mere speculation. In other words, Ms. Horrible Harriet Hare realizes that her former students, including the chief of police, have not learned deeply what she has intended to teach them. They have all been surface learners. They have forgotten what Ms. Hare has taught them. They are unable to transfer the critical thinking skills that she has lectured about and apply them to a real-life-situation outside school.

In *The Lord of the Flies* (Hook, 1990), several school-age boys, together with the injured pilot, are stranded on a paradisiacal and uninhabited island after a plane crash. Since the pilot—the only adult—is severely wounded, the children have no choice but to explore the island by themselves. Motivated by their desire to survive, the boys learn to swim, hunt, fish, gather food, build shelters, cook, pluck birds, tie knots, and make a fire. The older and more mature boys, Ralph and Jack, tell the other boys stories that amaze and intrigue them. But no one lectures. The boys do not have to repeat what others say. No one grade the boys, either. They learn by themselves in a free and motivating environment. They set their own goals and solve the problems that they encounter in their quest for survival. After a fight, a group of boys—the hunters—move to the other side of the island and build a new shelter. This time, it is bigger and more comfortable. They improve the skills they have recently learned. For example, they learn new techniques to hunt pigs and to catch fish. They even reflect, revisit, and question some of the stories that adults have told them before the airplane accident. Equally important, they can transfer the skills that they have learned from one situation to another. For example, Jack intends to build a fort by using—and improving—the techniques they all learned while building the shelters.

Throughout their time on the island, the boys never forget the skills, knowledge, and competences that they have learned. They boys are all deep learners. They can transfer skills they learn for one project to another. They can solve problems all the time by employing skills previously learned. And they change some of the skills and knowledge they have in order to solve new problems. They also reflect about their learning process. They are highly motivated, and they learn fast.

As briefly anticipated in the previous chapter, there are two main approaches to learning: deep learning and surface learning. Deep learning is a committed attitude to learning where learners learn for life. Deep learners never forget what they learn. They can transfer knowledge and skills to new situations and can apply what they learn to new contexts. They can solve problems they have never encountered. They understand the implications, applications, and consequences of what they learn. They can judge and critically evaluate what they learn (Bain, 2004).

Surface learning is a superficial approach to learning where students use knowledge that they acquire for a specific task, such as writing exams or papers, and once that task is done, they soon forget what they learn. Surface learners are not committed to their learning process. They are passive learners who simply absorb information that teachers or books transmit to them. Surface learners cannot use what they learn to solve unfamiliar problems, or to transfer their knowledge to other contexts. They cannot see beyond the information that they receive from their teachers or books. They cannot read between lines or beyond lines. They are unable to hypothesize about what they learn and to see its consequences, implications, and applications.

Like the boys stranded on the island, students can learn deeply, write deeply, read deeply, and engage in any academic, professional, or even everyday-life task in a deep way. Similarly, like Ms. Hare's students, learners can approach any task in a surface way.

A learner can also approach one aspect of a discipline in a surface way and another aspect of the discipline in a deep way. A learner can also take a deep approach to an aspect of the discipline at one time, and at another time he or she can take a surface approach to that same aspect of the discipline. For example, whereas Jack's hunters learn most skills deeply, their knowledge about the law on the island was superficial. Although Jack was a good mentor for helping the children discover knowledge in most areas and develop a wide array of important skills for their survival, when it came to the law on the island, his mentoring style changed radically. Like Ms. Hare with low grades and punishment, Jack also uses fear to encourage them to learn rules. He believes that fear will make the children learn for life about law. Not surprisingly, the hunters end up breaking the rules, which results in fatal consequences.

2.3   THE WAY WE TEACH: SIGNATURE PEDAGOGIES

Approaching an endeavor in a deep or surface way is an unconscious decision. It depends on many different factors such as the learning conditions, students' perceptions of those conditions, the learning environment, teachers' attitude, educational history, motivation, and cultural capital, among others. The factor that has the most influence on students'—unconscious—decision to take a deep or a surface approach to learning is the way we teach. When the boys on the island were free to explore and discover knowledge by themselves, they learned deeply. When Ms. Horrible Harriet Hare lectured and used fear and low grades to motivate students, they learned only superficially.

Most of us teach our disciplines in a very similar way, which is referred to as the signature pedagogy. A signature pedagogy is the predominant teaching method in a program of study across a certain geographical area (Shulman, 2004). Pedagogy is understood in a broad way to include the interactions between teacher and students, the setting, the learning environment, evaluation, and assignments given to students.

Several factors contribute to the widespread adoption of a similar teaching method in a discipline. These include the influence of elite higher education institutions that educate most leading professors, the influence of accrediting agencies that insist that teachers teach in a certain way, and tradition, that is to say, teachers follow the teaching method through which they were taught. Even popular culture plays a role by perpetuating the images of what law school and university teachers should do and look like in class. Unfortunately, the signature pedagogies in law school and criminal justice programs tend to create learning conditions that promote student surface learning.

2.4   THE CASE-DIALOGUE METHOD

In United States law schools, the predominant teaching pedagogy is the case-dialogue method introduced by Harvard Law School dean Christopher Columbus Langdell in the 1870s and immortalized by John Houseman's personification of Professor Kingsley in *The Paper Chase* (1973) directed by James Bridges[1].

The case-dialogue method is based on the dissection of edited appellate court cases contained in books known as casebooks. These cases contain the facts, the court's analysis, and decision. Additionally, they usually include questions about the case and other references. Students are expected to read the cases before class. Unlike the case method and problem-based learning pedagogies used in other programs such as business and medicine where students actually have to solve a problem, students do not solve any problem when reading the cases from the casebook. The case already contains the analysis and resolution by the court. In class, the teacher asks students questions about the cases. The teacher usually starts by asking a student to summarize the facts of the case. Then, the teacher asks the same student or another one to explain the court's analysis and decision. The bulk of the class is devoted to hypothetical questions about variations of the case and other hypothetical cases about the same legal topic that the teacher makes up or that the teacher borrowed from books, guides, or websites that offer resources for the law teacher. Students answer these questions, and the teacher follows up with new questions about the same hypothetical case or a new one. No one makes any conclusion or summarizes the law, which students have to come up with on their own or in groups outside class when they prepare for the final exam.

Since the 1980's, North American law schools have been gradually shifting the conception of the law "from a unitary, doctrine-focused, and homogeneous system to a more diversified, open, and plural process, where there is a relatively higher degree of tolerance for alternative perspectives and for the contribution of other disciplines" (Stein, 1991). Although this change in the legal paradigm implied a devaluation of Langdell's case-dialogue method in academic circles, and despite the efforts of many faculty members and authors in North America, law teaching

---

[1]Although this method derives both from a modified version of the Socratic dialogue and a variation of the case method, the case-dialogue method has little to do with the true spirit of the Socratic method. Unlike the case-dialogue method, the original Socratic method is a shared "dialogue between teacher and students in which both are responsible for pushing the dialogue forward through questioning. The dialogue facilitator asks probing questions in an effort to expose the values and beliefs which frame and support the thoughts and statements of the participants in the inquiry. The inquiry progresses interactively, and the teacher is as much a participant as a guide of the discussion. Furthermore, the inquiry is open-ended. There is no pre-determined argument or terminus to which the teacher attempts to lead the students" (Reich, 2003).

methodologies persist in following the case-dialogue method in its traditional form or with slight variations (Weston and Cranton, 1986).

2.5 LECTURES

A lecture consists of the teacher's transmission of knowledge to students, whose role is reduced to taking down notes, asking a few clarification questions, and reproducing the information in the form of exams and essays.

Lectures originated in early medieval universities where books were scarce. Practically speaking, only teachers had access to books. So, they transmitted the information from the books to their students in class. Teachers either read directly from the books to their students or recounted the information from those books orally. Students had to absorb and remember that information. Teachers made sure that their students knew the content of the books and the information transmitted in class by asking students questions where they had to reproduce that information back to their teachers.

Despite wide access to books, articles, and other publications both in print and in electronic form, the essence of lectures in today's higher education system has not changed considerably. Teachers continue to convey information orally to students about content that they read from books and other publications.

The lecture is the signature pedagogy for the teaching of law in Canada and Europe and for the teaching of criminal justice in undergraduate programs. In Canada, law schools claim to follow the American case-dialogue method. However, empirical analysis of what happens in the law school classroom reveals that the predominant teaching method is the lecture (Rochette, 2010). Most of these lectures focus—albeit not exclusively—on cases. Like in the United States, Canadian law school students also read casebooks that are modeled after the American counterparts. In Europe and elsewhere, lectures about the law (and not necessarily about cases) predominate. European law books, outside the common law world, focus more on the explanation of the law and principles rather than on judicial decisions. Criminal justice undergraduate programs both in North America and Europe, as well as in other regions, are based on lectures, where teachers explain all aspects of the criminal justice system.

2.6   SEMINARS

Some graduate programs in criminal justice focus on seminars. In other programs, teachers use lectures or a combination of lectures and seminars. In seminars, the teacher selects and assigns texts for students to read individually and then discuss in small groups, after which each group reports its discussions to the whole class. Then, the whole class engages in a discussion about the assigned texts.

In the seminar, "the teacher tries to serve mainly as a mediator and guide to a conversation among students themselves. A seminar instructor usually asks questions of students, at least at the beginning of class, but less to elicit particular answers and lead the class along a rigidly predetermined path than to stimulate conversation and debate among the students" (Brinkley et al, 1999).

2.7   ANALYSIS OF SIGNATURE PEDAGOGIES

There are several theoretical categories of analysis to examine the predominant pedagogy in a program. Bruffee (1999) distinguishes two types of teaching practices: lecture conventions and recitation conventions. In the lecture convention pedagogy, which includes traditional lectures, question-and-answer discussions, the case-dialogue method, and some types of lab sessions, teachers are the center of the teaching practice. Teachers are seen as the knowledge authority, and students' answers, questions, and participation reinforce this role of the teacher as expert. Teachers control the classroom interactions. And teachers evaluate students' learning. In this context, students are unable to discover and construct knowledge. In the lecture, only the teacher uses higher order cognitive skills and competences to prepare and deliver the lecture. Students use lower order cognitive skills, such as listening passively, taking notes, and reproducing information. The teacher robs students the possibility of negotiating knowledge among their peers. In the case-dialogue method, the teacher's complete control of the pedagogical exchanges deprives students of the freedom needed to engage in a deep learning process and the possibility to construct and negotiate knowledge with their own peers.

The recitation convention includes seminars, tutorials, and writing seminars, where students present their work to the teacher, who still controls, evaluates, and performs. The nature and knowledge authority vested in the teacher and the classroom's hierarchical social structure remain unquestioned. Students, even when purportedly talking to other students or commenting on other students' work, are actually performing for the teacher. Their contributions are influenced by students' perceptions of the teacher's requirements. Furthermore, the teacher retains the prerogative to lecture at any time, even if he or she does it subtly while commenting on a student's paper, answering a question, or giving instructions.

Critics of the seminar method argue that teachers do not help students discover and construct knowledge by themselves and do not help students engage in the practices that members of the professional or academic communities that students are trying to join routinely carry out. Despite a misperception that this method fosters active learning, in practice the discussion is a substitute for the lecture.

Many of my seminars as a graduate student were run by what I call the beach-ball method: Just as a crowd at an arena bounces a beach ball at random from one person to another, the professor depends on the students to keep the seminar going just by talking—which they do, bouncing from topic to topic without design (Cassuto, 2003).

Anton Rosenthal describes his discontent with this method as follows:

I was dissatisfied with the way I was teaching graduate seminars. The model for our department was somewhat unstated but dominant: select a number of readings relevant to the topic, bunch those books and articles together in topical groups, sit around and talk about them on the assigned class day, and have students write a 20 to 30-page cumulative paper (Rosenthal, 2005).

Usually, teachers select too many articles for students to read and include too much information in the seminars in the belief that quantity and difficulty of reading assignments will magically translate into learning. Then, they ask students to discuss their readings without actually doing anything with what they read other than to write a paper at the end of the course.

Both lecture conventions and recitation conventions are considered to lead to surface learning, because they do not create an environment where students can formulate their own goals and engage in a process of construction of knowledge through individual discovery and social interaction.

Another theoretical approach to examine the signature pedagogy in law school and criminal justice programs is Shulman's four dimensional analysis (Shulman, 2004). Any signature pedagogy has four dimensions: (1) surface structure, (2) deep structure, (3) tacit structure, and (4) shadow structure (Shulman, 2004). The surface structure of a pedagogy is the set of behaviors that can be observed. The deep structure is the set of underlying intentions and goals that the observable behavior models. The tacit structure refers to the values and dispositions that the behavior implicitly models. The shadow structure is the repressed pedagogy. It is what the pedagogy does not do.

The surface structure of a traditional lecture reveals that the teacher explains facts, students take notes and ask questions, and the teacher answers those questions. The deep structure of the traditional lecture is that there is an expert, the teacher, who has the knowledge and transmits it to nonexperts, the students. The tacit structure of the traditional lecture reveals that it promotes a foundational conception of knowledge as a real entity that is not subject to collective negotiation (Bruffee, 1999). The shadow structure of the lecture shows that it does not promote student research or student collaboration, students' formulation of goals, students' selection of problems or reading materials, students' initiatives, and self-evaluation, among many other equally important factors.

Similarly, the surface structure of the seminar shows that students read authoritative texts written by disciplinary experts and discuss them in small groups, which is followed by a whole class discussion facilitated by their teacher. The deep structure reveals that there is an expert, the author, who transmits knowledge to students through the texts that another disciplinary expert—the teacher—selects. The tacit structure shows that knowledge is a real entity which is transmitted to students from books and mediated by teacher-facilitated discussions. The shadow structure demonstrates that the teacher retains control of the class, that students' initiatives and creativity are suppressed, that self-evaluation and metacognition are not present, and that students do not engage in problem solving, among other issues.

The surface structure of the case-dialogue method is a series of oral questions that the teacher asks his or her students about edited appellate cases and hypothetical cases which the students answer orally. The deep structure is the dissection of cases through the rule-based analysis of judicial cases. The tacit structure shows that there is an unquestioned acceptance and respect for authority, whether it is the law teacher (in the teacher–student relation), the judge (in the trial setting), the lawyer (with respect to the lawyer–client relation), or the precedent (as the unquestioned source of law in the common law world). The shadow structure shows that students do not engage in research, collaborative learning, extensive writing, consultation of texts about law written outside the legal field, the production of media texts, the analysis of popular culture stories, the drafting of legal documents, the negotiation of deals, the learning of law that does not emanate from governmental authority, and the examination of comparative law solutions, among many other issues. Like the shadow structure of lectures and seminars, it also shows that students lack initiative and power in most aspects of the class.

Shulman's (2004) four-dimensional categories of analysis lead to the same results as Bruffee's framework for analysis, that is to say that, the case-dialogue method, the lectures, and the seminars do not help create an environment that is conducive to deep learning, because they fail to promote the conditions that encourage students to embark on a deep learning process.

2.8 NOTION OF DEEP LEARNING

Deep learning is a complex process of permanent knowledge construction. It takes place when a learner faces an exciting problem or question that is processed in story format (Bain, 2004). This problem, question, or situation referred to as input story, creates a cognitive conflict derived from social interaction with peers that the learner feels motivated to solve. To do so, the learner makes—non-arbitrary and substantive—connections between new knowledge arising from the input story (which must be within the learner's zone of proximal development) and knowledge that the learner already has, which is also stored in story format and which is part of the learner's cognitive structure (activated existing story). While making these connections individually and together with peers, the learner employs higher order cognitive and metacognitive skills, processes, and competences. If adequately and intrinsically motivated by the input story, the learner will change his or her cognitive structure so as to resolve the cognitive conflict. In so doing, the learner will incorporate the new knowledge into his or her cognitive structure, which will produce a conceptual change, that is, a new schema or the modification of an existing one, which will also be stored in story format. The learner will be able to use and apply this knowledge to new and unfamiliar situations and see the connections to a larger framework. At the same time, at the social level, this process implies one of the following changes: a reacculturation from one community of knowledge to another (Bruffee, 1999), or a movement from the periphery of an academic or professional community to its center, where the learner achieves full participation by performing the roles and functions that experts (lawyers and criminal justice professionals in the legal and criminal justice fields) display in the community (Lave and Wenger, 1991). For deep learning to occur, there must also be an ongoing evaluation and self-evaluation of the learning process and an awareness of this movement and the resulting conceptual change (Piaget, 1969)[2].

2.9   NOTION OF POPULAR CULTURE

Before breaking down the notion of deep learning into its main elements, let's briefly analyze the concept of popular culture and its connection to the deep learning process. Strictly speaking, popular culture is not an element of the deep learning process, but it can greatly maximize it by permeating the whole process.

There is an important theoretical debate about the definition of popular culture. Most of this debate revolves around the distinction between popular culture and high culture. In most cases, popular culture is defined as whatever is left once you have defined high culture. In this sense, it is a residual category (Storey, 2001). With the advent of postmodernism, the boundaries between high and popular culture have blurred (Jameson, 1991). Other definitions focus on the massive aspect of popular culture, whether it is the massive receptivity of popular culture texts and practices

---

[2]Piaget (1969) explained this process of conceptual change by means of the assimilation and accommodation principles. Individuals receive continuous stimuli from the environment, which causes disequilibrium. Individuals will assimilate that stimulus and incorporate it into their previously existing cognitive structures. This process, known as assimilation, is subjective, because human beings tend to modify experience or information to fit it in with pre-existing beliefs. But continuous stimuli from the environment cause disequilibrium, as the cognitive structures that individuals use to respond to these stimuli are not useful any more. Thus, there is an adaptation process, that is, the individual tries to assimilate the input story to the existing cognitive structures that he or she has and accommodates such structures to the new situations. Accommodation involves altering existing schemas, or ideas, as a result of new information or new experiences. New schemas may also be developed during this process (Sanjurjo and Vera, 1994).

among the general public (Bennett, 1980) or the massive production of these texts (Ross, 1989). Other notions of popular culture emphasize the political aspects of this concept. They define it as a terrain of exchange and negotiation between the ruling class and the working class (Gramsci, 2000). Another line of theorists conceive of popular culture as "an empty conceptual category, one which can be filled in a wide variety of often conflicting ways, depending on the context of use" (Storey, 2001).

Without ignoring the political aspects of the notion of popular culture, I adopt Storey's conception and fill that void with all cultural texts (and practices), whether their production is artisanal or large-scale. In this sense, it includes films (features, documentaries, shorts, and home videos uploaded to online sites), TV shows (comedies, dramas, reality shows, talk shows, and news programs), theater plays, books, magazines, newspapers, songs, commercials, radio shows, video games, applications, and pictures, among many other cultural texts.

2.10   POPULAR CULTURE AND THE DEEP LEARNING PROCESS

At a general level, popular culture has a pedagogical aspect that "raises important questions regarding such issues as the relevance of everyday life, the importance of student voice, the significance of both meaning and pleasure in the learning process, and the relationship between knowledge and power in the curriculum" (Giroux and Simon, 1988). Furthermore, popular culture helps understand the world around us and construct our identities (Williams, 2012). It provides us with stories, examples, anecdotes, symbols, characters, voices, and landscapes to connect to the world and make sense of it. Popular culture also gives visibility to many people located at society's margins, who have traditionally been excluded from higher education. It legitimates and transmits the language, codes, and values of non-elite groups. We identify with popular culture stories, as they reflect our experiences and beliefs. And at the same time, popular culture stories contribute to define our own experiences, values, and perspectives.

Despite its importance in everyday, social, and professional settings, popular culture has been relegated in educational organizations.

The dominant discourse, in short, devalues pedagogy as a form of cultural production and it likewise scorns popular culture. Needless to say, while popular culture is generally ignored in the schools, it is not an insignificant force in shaping how students view themselves and their own relations to various forms of pedagogy and learning. […] Popular culture and pedagogy represent important terrains of cultural struggle which offer both subversive discourses and important theoretical elements through which it becomes possible to rethink as a viable and important form of cultural politics (Giroux and Simon, 1988).

Apart from all these general reasons, popular culture plays a very concrete role in helping advance the teaching and learning process. As will be discussed throughout the book, given the appropriate teacher's intervention, popular culture can foster the activation of students' cognitive structures and the development of intellectual skills at a level not always possible without recourse to popular culture (Chapter 2). It also facilitates the development and refinement of cognitive skills that are difficult to learn in traditional teaching and learning settings such as rapid cognitive process and strategies (Chapter 3). Popular culture provides a powerful means to construct and negotiate knowledge (Chapter 2). It also constitutes an important tool to reflect about substantive aspects of academic disciplines such as law and criminal justice (Chapter 5). It helps students understand academic disciplines at a profound level, and it helps students become aware of their learning process (Chapter 7) and learning achievements (Chapter 8). It also helps motivate students intrinsically to engage in the learning process (Chapter 4). Additionally, popular culture helps define academic disciplines such as law and criminal justice (Chapter 5). It also shapes professional fields, including law and criminal justice, affecting the expectations of their professional agents and laypersons alike, the professional practice itself, and even the outcome of particular cases (Chapter 5). Furthermore, the production of popular culture provides a unique opportunity to improve professional practice (Chapter 6) and to move to the center of academic and professional communities (Chapter 2).

It becomes our responsibility, then, as educators, to prepare our students/citizens, to learn how to use, consume, and to have personal power over the media. Empowerment comes when we are able to read media and make informed decisions about what we have read (Reynolds, 2012).

2.11 THE DEEP LEARNING STORY AND ITS ELEMENTS

People think in terms of stories. They understand the world in terms of stories that they have already understood. New events or problems are understood by reference to old previously understood stories and explained to others by the use of stories. We understand personal problems and relationships between people through stories that typify those situations. We also understand just about everything else this way as well (Schank, 2000).

There are several layers of stories when it comes to the deep learning process. First, you can think of the deep learning process as a story itself. Second, the deep learning process contains several stories, mainly the input story, which is the central aspect of the process, and the existing stories, that are stored in the learners' mind. Third, every aspect of the deep learning process is also understood and processed as a story.

I will use the story metaphor to discuss the deep learning process. The deep learning story shares its basic organization with the narrative structure that predominates in popular culture stories. This structure consists of: (1) setup, which introduces the characters, settings, and background; (2) the conflict, which causes tension to the protagonist, creates a crisis, includes actions that the protagonist takes to deal with the conflict, and the protagonist's interactions with others; and (3) the resolution of the conflict, which resolves the crisis and restores balance to the protagonist's life. The elements of the deep learning process are: (1) the input story, that is, a problem, question, or situation within the learner's zone of proximal development; (2) the story conflict, that is, the cognitive conflict and the series of higher order cognitive skills, competences, and processes that the learner engages with individually and collectively; and (3) the resolution of the conflict, i.e., both the conceptual change and the changes in or across academic and professional communities. Like good popular culture stories that do not end on the last page of the book or with the last frame of a film but that are interpreted and reflected upon by the reader or viewer, the deep learning process also includes an element of interpretation referred to as evaluation and metacognitive reflection (Table 2.1).

If any aspect of this complex process does not occur, or if, in other words, any of the elements are not present, students do not learn deeply. Their learning will be merely superficial. They will be unable to remember, transfer, and apply what they learn to new activities and situations.

2.11.1   THE INPUT STORY

The deep learning story begins with the input story, which consists of a problem, a question, or a situation for the learner to grapple with (Bain, 2004). The input story introduces new knowledge about the discipline or task that students are trying to learn, such as any aspect of law or criminal justice, and it sets the whole learning process into motion (Bain, 2004). For example, in *Other Desert Cities* (Baitz, 2010) a play directed by Robert Egan, the question "What happened to him?" resounds in Brooke Wyeth's mind and guides all her writing process of a novel based on her brother's suicide. She ponders this question for a while and decides to go back home for the first time in 6 years in search for an answer. This question will remain in her head while she embarks upon a journey that will eventually lead to a profound change in her life. In *The Exorcist* (1973), directed by William Friedkin, Chris McNeil faces a desperate problem that will make her revisit her longstanding religious position in order to find a solution for her daughter. Chris's daughter, Regan McNeil suffers inexplicable physical and personality transformations. When she sees that physicians and psychiatrists are unable to find a cure for Regan, Chris, an atheist, re-examines her beliefs and seeks the services of a priest to perform an exorcism on her daughter.

An effective input story shocks, perplexes, amazes, or intrigues the learner, who, as a consequence, becomes fully immersed in the learning process. Furthermore, effective input stories "are authentic: they seem important to students and are similar to those that professionals in the field might undertake" (Bain, 2004). An input story is also effective when teachers help students see its significance and connection to both issues that students are already interested in and issues of social, cultural, and personal significance beyond the discipline (Bain, 2004).

In order to help advance the deep learning process, the input story must contain new knowledge that is within the learner's zone of proximal development. There is a level of effective development, which is what the learner can do independently and a level of potential development, which is constituted by what the individual is capable of doing with the help of other adults or more capable peers. The distance between effective development and potential development is the "zone of proximal development" (Vygotsky, 1978). Learning takes place when knowledge is within students' zone of proximal development (Vygotsky, 1978). If it is within the level of effective development, students can deal with that knowledge without having to change their cognitive structures. If knowledge is beyond their zone of proximal development, students will be unable to comprehend it and will not be capable to change their cognitive structures. For example, when discussing the theory of offense in criminal law, it is difficult for students to understand the notion of attendant circumstances if the other types of social harm (wrongful result and wrongful conduct) are not yet part of their cognitive structures[3]. In *The Lord of the Flies* (Hook, 1990), because the twins' cognitive structures lack many of the stories about aerial battles, they do not understand why a pilot may have parachuted down the island, so they mistake the pilot for a beast.

2.11.2   THE STORY CONFLICT: THE COGNITIVE CONFLICT

The deep learning story conflict includes the challenges and obstacles that the learner faces, known as the cognitive conflict, which constitutes the driving force that impels the process toward its resolution, and the actions that the learner takes individually and together with peers in order to overcome those challenges.

The cognitive conflict in the deep learning process is an internal conflict where the learner is at odds with himself or herself. It is a situation in which the attempt to explain the new knowledge by means of the existing cognitive structures leads to faulty expectations (Bain, 2004). The cognitive conflict generates an imbalance in the learner's knowledge structure (Pozo, 2008). This is produced when the learner's cognitive structure does not coincide with, or cannot explain, the new knowledge in the input story, or cannot explain it in a coherent way. To solve the conflict, the learner creates responses, asks questions, investigates, and discovers until the

---

[3]Social harm is the negation, endangering, or destruction of a socially valuable and legally protected interest, whether individual, societal, or state. It may adopt the form of a wrongful result, wrongful conduct, or attendant circumstances. Social harm is expressed as a wrongful result when the offence is defined in terms of a prohibited result. Social harm takes the form of wrongful conduct when the offence is described in terms of injurious conduct, and no harmful result is required, such as the case of possession of prohibited firearms. In this case, the social interest—to live peacefully without perils that may be triggered by the use of firearms—is endangered by the possession of illegal firearms. The definition of an offence may include other elements defined as attendant circumstances. An example of attendant circumstances can be found in the offence of bribery, which takes place when a judicial officer or a member of a legislature corruptly accepts money. The acceptance of money only by those who hold such offices constitutes the social harm in the bribery offence. Thus, judicial and legislative officers are the attendant circumstance, whose corruption constitutes social harm.

learner constructs knowledge that restores that balance (Carretero, 2009; Pozo, 2008).

The default student attitude to the input story is to adopt a surface approach by ignoring the conflict, or by trying to make it fit somehow within their existing cognitive structures (Bain, 2004). This is because we all have a tendency to try to understand new information in terms of existing knowledge (Bain, 2004), just like Ms. Horrible Harriet Hare's students did with Boss Baker's explanation that the thief had a stained red shawl. Since Tiny Tessie wore a red shawl the next morning, then she had to be the thief. This story is easy to understand. It does not require changing anyone's cognitive structure.

> When we need to explain something to ourselves, which happens every time we fail to understand something, we choose, if we can, a standard explanation, and we try to adapt it to our current situation. [...] We rely upon familiar explanations because we can find them easily, and similarly, others will easily accept such explanations because they are also familiar with them (Schank, 1986).

Rapunzel's tale (Grimm and Grimm, 1884) also helps illustrate how the cognitive conflict works. A witch has locked Rapunzel in a room at the top of a tower in the middle of the woods. The tower has no stairs and no door. There is only a window in the room. At first, Rapunzel tries to escape. She tries to push down a wall by kicking and punching it, but the wall is too hard for her. She makes several attempts, but she is not successful. Then, she gives up and convinces herself that she cannot escape. Trying to escape is a conflict (albeit not an academic one) that Rapunzel has tried to solve always in the same way. Instead of trying a different approach (shouting, using her own hair to climb down the window, jumping off the window, getting out with the witch when she comes to visit her), Rapunzel has ignored the conflict and has resigned to live in a locked room with no contact with the outside world. She does not try to modify her preconceived idea that trying to push down a wall is the only way to escape from an apartment[4].

---

[4]Furthermore, the actual cognitive conflict in the deep learning process is produced through interaction with the social context (Vygotsky, 1978). In Rapunzel's example, she probably failed to change her cognitive structure because the cognitive conflict did not arise from, and did not even have, a collective instance. Later in the story, we learn that only after Rapunzel interacts with a prince does she succeed to escape.

Such outcome results because, as discussed above, we all have a tendency to try to understand new information in terms of existing knowledge (Bain, 2004). But students can instead take a deep approach to learning if they modify their cognitive structures while working to solve the problem or situation. For this to occur, learners must actually care that their cognitive structures cannot help them deal with the problem, question, or situation in the input story (Bain, 2004). As discussed in Chapter 4, students must be motivated enough to try to solve the problem. Otherwise, they will not change their existing cognitive structures.

2.11.3   THE STORY CONFLICT: NONARBITRARY AND SUBSTANTIVE HIGHER ORDER COGNITIVE SKILLS, COMPETENCES, AND PROCESSES

In order to resolve the cognitive conflict, the deep learner makes meaningful, nonarbitrary, and substantive connections between the input story and another story that the input story activates from the learner's own cognitive structure, which is referred to as the existing story or the activated existing story. A motivating input story makes the learner search through his or her repertoire of existing stories, which are indexed in the learner's brain according to convenient labels, and select the one that best links to the input story[5]. In biological terms, a learner receives input from the outside world through the brain's sensory cortex. This input is transmitted to the back integrative cortex, which integrates sensory information to create images and meaning. Then, the frontal integrative cortex analyzes these images, solves the problem, and comes up with a solution (Zull, 2002). As a way of illustration, suppose that in a criminal justice class you ask your students the following question: "Do you think that the main role of the prosecutor in a criminal trial should be to seek a conviction or to arrive at the truth?" This question may activate different stories in students' minds. Some may connect it to a popular culture show that they indexed in their minds as "prosecutor and convictions". Others may connect it to a particular aspect of a reading they did for the class. Yet, other students may connect it to a TV show that they indexed as "criminal

---

[5]From the information received from the input story, the learner selects only what is relevant for the activated, existing knowledge, and discards the irrelevant. Then, from this selected information, the learner makes abstractions and generalizes its meaning (Carretero, 2009).

trial". Some other students may have had a personal experience with a prosecutor in a criminal trial and may connect the question in the input story to that experience. The richer their readings, experiences, and prior knowledge, the more meaningful the connections will be.

In the deep learning process, the learner makes this connection between the new knowledge arising from the input story and the existing story by engaging in a series of higher order cognitive skills, competences, and processes. These skills, processes, and competences include critical analysis, synthesis, problem solving, extrapolation, theorization, comparison, contrast, evaluation, and rapid cognition, among others. For example, in *Manhattan* (Allen, 1979), Mary Wilke discusses art with Isaac. While listening to Isaac praise the Castelli photographic exhibition (input story), Mary searches through her repertoire of existing stories and selects the story of Diane Arbus photography. Mary compares Castelli's work with that of Arbus. She can identify those aspects of Arbus' photographs that are absent in Castelli's works. Mary critically evaluates Castelli's works. She hypothesizes about the quality of his works and reaches a conclusion about the artistic value of Castelli's exhibition. These are all higher order processes that are directly related to the input story and that will lead to deep learning about art and photography, provided the other aspects of the process are present. In contrast, when Ms. Horrible Harriet Hare lectures her students, they simply listen to her explanations and take down notes, which they will later memorize and reproduce back to her. The competences that students use to make connections, if any, to Ms. Hare's input story are low-order. Thus, learning is a consequence of thinking, and "knowledge comes on the coattails of thinking. As we think about and with the content that we are learning, we truly learn it" (Perkins, 2009)[6].

---

[6]There are many lists and taxonomies that help us classify these skills, competences, and processes. Bloom's taxonomy is the most widely used set of cognitive skills. The higher levels of Bloom's taxonomy (application, analysis, synthesis, and evaluation) may help promote deep learning (Bloom, 1984). Roger Schkank came up with the 12 cognitive processes that are considered essential for a good education. These are: conceptual processes: (1) prediction, (2) modeling, (3) experimentation, (4) evaluation, analytic processes: (5) diagnosis, (6) planning, (7) causation, (8) judgment, social processes: (9) influence, (10) teamwork, (11) negotiation, and (12) describing. Similarly, Biggs and Tang (2007) classify these competences as those that merely help increase knowledge, which they refer to as quantitative and those that help deepen understanding, which are qualitative in nature. Quantitative competences include identifying, doing simple procedures, enumerating, describing, listing, combining, and doing algorithms, among others. Qualitative competences include comparing, contrasting, explaining causes, analyzing, relating, applying, theorizing, generalizing, hypothesizing, and reflecting. Quantitative competences usually lead to superficial learning, whereas qualitative ones may lead to deep learning (Biggs and Tang, 2007).

2.11.4   THE STORY CONFLICT: COLLECTIVE NEGOTIATION OF MEANINGS AND SOCIAL INTERACTION

Like in most popular culture stories, the protagonist does not work alone. The deep learner also interacts with peers in order to solve the cognitive conflict, as it cannot be resolved by the individual learner alone.

Learning is both an individual and a collective enterprise. Learning requires individual cognitive and metacognitive processes. All higher order cognitive processes, for example, communication, language, and reasoning, are first acquired in a social context and are later internalized (Carretero, 2009). We have the capacity to reflect and think, that is, to employ higher order cognitive and metacognitive processes and competences on an individual basis, because we have previously internalized social conversations (Vygotsky, 1978). "We learn together by analyzing the related experiences of others to arrive at a common understanding that holds until new evidence or arguments present themselves" (Mezirow, 1991). Thus, the deep learner constructs and reconstructs knowledge by engaging in conversations with peers through the use of higher order cognitive processes, skills, and competences. In *The Lord of the Flies* (Hook, 1980), the boys, most notably Ralph and Piggy, converse about their learning process all the time. They vividly discuss and compare fishing techniques; they talk about ways to improve their health by eating more protein. They also revisit the input stories that they received from adults before the plane crash, they question, and challenge them together. The boys negotiate their understanding of life, death, and other fundamental issues. Without these collective negotiations, their learning would be superficial.

There is a strong—albeit not necessarily evident at first glance—connection between diversity and deep learning. Since the deep learning process requires a cognitive conflict that is generated through social interaction with peers (Vygotsky, 1978) who are at different developmental stages (Magolda, 2002; Perry, 1970), when the learner interacts with peers who have very different backgrounds, the exploration of the problem, question, or situation that the learner is trying to solve, answer, or deal with will be richer than if he or she only interacts with peers who come from the same cultural background. Law school and university admissions committees generally know this and try to come up with incoming classes that reflect a widely diverse demographic composition. But diversity can only play this role in the deep learning process if teachers actively and explicitly recognize and incorporate diverse worldview perspectives into the classroom. If, on the contrary, even when there is a diverse group of students, teachers repress students' backgrounds, experiences, and cultures, they insist on teaching from a single cultural perspective, and they reject diverse ways of generating and expressing thought, then the cognitive conflict and the conceptual change (if it happens) will be significantly poorer.

2.11.5   THE RESOLUTION OF THE CONFLICT: THE CONCEPTUAL CHANGE AND CHANGES IN THE SOCIAL POSITION

In most popular culture stories, after struggling with a problem, question, or situation, the protagonist achieves his or her goal and grows. In the deep learning process, the resolution of the cognitive conflict leads to individual and social changes. At the individual level, it gives rise to the conceptual change. Conceptual change is a change in the learner's cognitive structure. Through interaction with new knowledge, learners come to incorporate that knowledge into their cognitive structures and change their cognitive structures forever. From a biological point of view, learning produces a physical change in the brain. The brain contains billions of neurons, which receive and transmit information in the form of chemical or electric signals to other neurons through synapses. These synapses, that is, the connections between neurons, form neuronal networks that wire the brain by building up on other neuronal networks. Synapses are formed in the brain in response to experiences and learning (Zull, 2002). There is "a neuronal network in our brain for everything we know" (Zull, 2002). A conceptual change resulting from a deep learning process forms unique connections between neuronal networks (Bransford et. al., 2008). The conceptual change is a change in neuronal connections: "more connections, stronger connections, different connections, or even fewer connections" (Zull, 2002). The existence of the conceptual change distinguishes the deep learning process from other forms of learning.

The resolution of the cognitive conflict also leads to changes in the learner's social position. All members in every academic or professional discipline share some common features about the way in which they interact within the discipline and the outside world. These common aspects include similar ways of thinking about the discipline, communicating with other members of the discipline, interpreting thought, reading academic or professional texts, writing texts, and communicating with laypeople. Most disciplines and professions also have smaller groups that are organized around geographical areas, specializations, or type of professional work, among others[7].

Deep learning implies—geographical—changes either across academic or professional communities or inside one's own community. The first possibility involves a process of moving from one academic or professional community, such as the community of law school students or the community of criminal justice students to another, such as the community of lawyers or the community of criminal justice professionals (Bruffee, 1999). Law school and university teachers help students leave their original communities and join their target communities by helping them acculturate in the linguistic and paralinguistic discourse of the professional or academic community that they try to join. The second possible consequence of deep learning at the social level involves moving from the periphery or margins of a community of knowledge to the center, where the learner achieves full participation by performing the roles and functions that experts display in the community (Lave and Wenger, 1991). When students transition from their original communities to join professional and academic communities of knowledge, they do so gradually. They observe the way their teachers talk, question, respond, and think. They also observe written disciplinary conventions. They interact with their peers. They negotiate meanings

---

[7]For example, these may include: (1) areas of specialization, such as criminal law, property law, torts law, contracts law; (2) geographical areas, the Chicago Council of Lawyers, Puerto Rican Bar Association, Canadian Bar Association; (3) ethnicity, for example, the Hispanic Lawyers Association of Illinois, the Chinese American Bar Association; (4) gender and sexual orientation, such as the National Association of Women Judges, the Lesbian and Gay Law Association of Greater New York; (5) their place of work or type of work, the National Association of University and College Attorneys, Association of Trial Lawyers of America, Federal Magistrate Judges Association; (6) a theory, such as the Critical Legal Studies Association, the Critical Criminology Working Group; or (7) any possible combination of these or other similar categories. Some subgroups can form subcommunities that may be small and close, whereas other groups can be very large and include professionals or academics from all over the world. Teaching for deep learning implies helping students become members of these academic or professional communities. In order to become full members of the communities they want to join, students need to master the general and specific categories of analysis, reading and writing styles, and strategies to communicate thought in writing and to interpret academic texts that predominate in these communities. For this purpose, it is important to recreate the whole world of that discipline or profession in the classroom, where students can try out all the activities that disciplinary or professional experts usually engage in, including those activities that are not traditionally considered strictly academic such as learning to negotiate fees, evaluating associates, or talking to the press (Perkins, 2002). This offers students the whole picture of the field and not just an artificially selected fraction.

within this community and construct knowledge. Eventually, they move to the center as they adopt the linguistic and paralinguistic language of the experts in the community. They embrace the beliefs, ideas, methods, and principles of the community.

A prominent student vividly recounts her transition from the margins of a community of dance students at Princeton University toward the center of the community of professional dancers, thanks to classes she took with renowned jazz dance teacher Frank Hatchett in Studio A.

> During university, […] I was accepted to a theater company that used quite a bit of dancing in its programs. The actors were divided into 'dancers-dancers' and the 'background dancers'. My dancing ability at the time solidified my position as a background dancer. I watched and envied the dancer group and vowed to one day become good enough to join it. The following summer I began taking classes with Frank Hatchett at the Broadway Dance Center. I took two to three classes a day and was determined to become an eligible dancer. […] My life changed the moment I walked into the back corner of Studio A. […] I would never have been able to perform eight shows a week on Broadway […]. From the back of Studio A to center stage to the wall at Sardi's, I have steadily been moving forward (Hatchett and Gitlin, 2000).

2.11.6   EVALUATION AND METACOGNITIVE REFLECTION

Just like good films, TV shows, and books that require an instance of interpretation and reflection, the deep learning process also requires reflection about the input story, the resulting conceptual and social position changes, and the steps taken toward the resolution of the cognitive conflict. This reflection is done mainly through metacognitive competences discussed in Chapter 7.

TABLE 2.1   The Deep Learning Process.

Deep learning process	
Elements	Meaning
The input story	Problem, question, or situation that the learner finds motivating.

TABLE 2.1   *(Continued)*

The story conflict: cognitive conflict	The challenges and obstacles that the learner faces, which constitute the driving force that impels the process toward its resolution and the actions that the learner takes individually and together with peers in order to overcome those challenges.
The story conflict: nonarbitrary and substantive higher order cognitive skills, competences, and processes	The meaningful, nonarbitrary, and substantive connections between the input story and another story that the input story activates from the learner's own cognitive structure (the activated existing story).
The story conflict: collective negotiation of meanings and social interaction	The learner's interaction with peers in order to solve the cognitive conflict, as it cannot be resolved by the individual learner alone.
The resolution of the conflict: the conceptual change and changes in the social position	A change in the learner's cognitive structure, i.e., the incorporation of new knowledge into the learner's cognitive structure and a change in the learner's social position (academic or professional disciplinary community).
Evaluation and metacognitive reflection	Reflection about the input story, the resulting conceptual and social position changes, and the steps taken toward the resolution of the cognitive conflict.

2.12   SUMMARY

A fixation with the case-dialogue method in United States law schools, the abuse of lectures in universities in North America and Europe, an obsession with seminar teaching in most criminal justice graduate programs, and a combination of the case-dialogue and lectures in Canadian law schools have given rise to superficial learning across the board, as these pedagogies deprive students of the possibility of discovering and constructing knowledge in authentic or recreated disciplinary environments.

Teaching for deep learning is the key to changing this problem. For deep learning to occur, the learner must face an exciting input story that contains a problem, question, or situation that gives rise to a cognitive conflict derived from interaction with peers and that the learner feels motivated to solve. To do so, the learner must make nonarbitrary and substantive connections between new knowledge arising from the input story and an activated story in the learner's existing cognitive structure through recourse to higher order cognitive and metacognitive competences. The new knowledge that the learner grapples with must be within the learner's zone of proximal development. If the input story is motivating, the learner will change his or her cognitive structure. This will produce two inter-related phenomena. At the individual level, the learner will produce a conceptual change. From a biological point of view, this change will imply a physical transformation of the neuronal connections in the learner's brain. At the social level, there will be a reacculturation from one community of knowledge to another or a movement from the periphery of an academic or professional community to its center. Deep learning also requires an awareness of this movement and the resulting conceptual change. Absent these phenomena, learning is merely superficial. In this case, students will forget what they learn once they take the exams and finish the course.

Popular culture plays a very important role in the whole deep learning process. It greatly maximizes the quality of students' learning by moti-vating students and by providing opportunities for students to develop higher order intellectual skills.

The next chapter focuses on how popular culture can promote rapid cognition thought processes. Rapid cognition, a skill generally devalued in higher education, is an important competence which lawyers and criminal justice officers rely upon in their daily professional practice. The chapter will analyze the main characteristics of rapid cognition and will discuss how popular culture can help students improve the effectiveness of their rapid cognition strategies and decisions.

KEYWORDS

- deep learning
- surface learning
- popular culture
- input story
- story conflict
- signature pedagogies

PART 2
Popular Culture

CHAPTER 3

Popular Culture and Rapid Cognition

Decisions based on emotion aren't decisions at all.
They're instincts. Which can be of value.
The rational and the irrational complement each other.
Individually they're far less powerful.

—House of Cards (2012)

ABSTRACT

Despite the importance of rapid cognition for professional and academic practice, it doesn't have room in the higher education curriculum, which places a disproportionate emphasis on critical thinking and other related thought processes. Rapid cognition is the fast processing of vast amounts of information, which results in an immediate conclusion. Rapid cognition processes can be educated and can be learned deeply. Popular culture stories offer a unique opportunity to teach students how to master rapid cognition effectively.

3.1 INTRODUCTION

There is a strong emphasis on critical thinking and other analytical thought processes in law schools and criminal justice programs. At the same time, there is a clear devalue of other ways of thinking, particularly rapid cognition. Rapid cognition consists of fast processing of vast amounts of information, which results in a speedy conclusion. Rapid cognition is associated with instinctive thinking; and it is responsible for most of the decisions we take in our personal, social, and professional lives.

Like other thought processes, rapid cognition processes can also be educated. They can be learned deeply. Popular culture plays a very significant role in helping students learn to improve the effectiveness of their rapid cognition processes and decisions. Popular culture stories offer multitude of examples of individuals using rapid cognition models, including literally thousands of situations involving lawyers and criminal justice professionals. They also give us the opportunity to see the results of decisions taken intuitively. This permits learners to reflect about rapid cognition and to fine tune their strategies taking into consideration what works and what does not. In turn, all this helps enrich the deep-learning process by providing students with a wide array of diverse intellectual skills, competences, and processes, which students can fully deploy in their future legal and criminal justice professions.

I will begin this chapter with an analysis of the concept of rapid cognition. Then, I will briefly discuss the emphasis on critical thinking skills in law schools and criminal justice programs. I will, then, examine how we can educate our students' use of rapid cognition strategies and the role that popular culture plays in rapid cognition.

3.2   RAPID COGNITION

In *Columbo* (1968–2003), after a very brief encounter with individuals who are both close and unrelated to the victim, Lieutenant Columbo (Peter Falk) instantly knows who committed the murder. He has an uncanny sense to identify the murderer through casual, unrelated, and even naïve questions. For example, in a *Trace of Murder* (S13 E2, 1997), directed by Vincent McEveety, after a quick glance at the victim's body, Columbo starts questioning LAPD forensic psychologist Patrick Kinsley (David Rasche) who is in the murder scene to investigate the homicide. Something tells Columbo that Kinsley is the murderer. He asks Kinley to join him in the investigation. He visits Kinsley several times. He asks him to interact with the victim's family and lawyers. Columbo wants to spend time with him because he senses that Kinsley killed the victim. In *Columbo*'s episode *Columbo Goes to College* (1990) directed by E. W. Swackhamer, lieutenant Columbo is invited to give a lecture in a criminology class at a local college. When a student asks him what the most important strategy to solve a crime is, he answers that he follows his nose. By smelling the crime scene, by scenting the fear of a suspect, by smelling the victim, lieutenant Columbo instantly finds out who committed the crime and how. Most of the cognitive processes we engage in consist of quick mental reactions and almost instinctive thinking (Kahneman, 2011). We take the majority of important decisions in our everyday and professional lives rapidly without embarking on what is usually referred to as critical thinking skills or analytical reasoning. Critical thinking is a conscious and carefully reasoned logical process of reaching a conclusion by carefully examining the evidence, claims, and arguments used to reach that conclusion. In most instances of our personal and professional lives, we quickly reach a conclusion in the first few seconds without ever engaging in this long process. In everyday language, we refer to this as intuition, first impression, first sight, or gut feeling. This is, in fact, a very complex process that takes place in the adaptive unconscious of our brains (Gladwell, 2007). This cognitive strategy—also known in the literature as System 1 thinking (Kahneman, 2011; Gladwell, 2007)—originates in the survival instinct developed by our ancestors, long before our species evolved into the human race. This strategy is closely connected to the fight-or-flee response that takes place in our brains when we perceive an attack or a threat. In those situations, we need to react quickly. We need to assess the situation very fast, make a decision, and act accordingly. In most cases in our daily lives, there is no harm or threat of harm. But our brain scans and processes a vast amount of information and makes very quick decisions based on the processed information. We use rapid cognition strategies to take most of our decisions in life, including professional decisions in the legal and criminal justice fields. These decisions range from asking someone out on a date to planning the best strategy to defend a client in a high-profile criminal case. For example, contrary to what may generally be assumed, hiring panels select a candidate during the first few minutes—or even seconds—of a job interview. Similarly, students evaluate their professors during the first minutes of the very first class. Empirical research shows that these evaluations seldom change after months or years as from the first encounter. Also, judges and jurors make decisions on whether an accused is guilty of a crime or a defendant is liable for damages after a few minutes of meeting the accused or the defendant.

In most of these cases, we do not realize that we have made the decision in minutes or even seconds. We are not generally aware of this process. This is because "our actions frequently precede our understanding of why we acted in particular ways. In other words, we use outcomes to make sense—at a conscious level—of what we have just done—at a subconscious level. We react first and then we think about our actions" (Hogarth, 2003). For example, in *Makers: Lisa Leslie* (2014), the first female basketball player to ever made a slam dunk, she tells the audience that she first "dunked it before she could realize that she had done so." Whereas Leslie is quite articulate, she is unable to explain how she dunked it.

Research studies show that when asked to explain our decisions, reactions, and thoughts we may come up with elaborate explanations which have little to do with the thought processes that actually took place in our brains. Gladwell (2011) recounts some research experiments with top athletes who were asked to explain their moves and plays. Their explanations simply did not match what they actually did. In *Columbo's A Trace of Murder* (1997), when a bartender asks Columbo how he solved the case, Columbo cannot explain why he has targeted Patrick Kinsley from the very beginning of the investigation. Columbo comes up with an elaborate explanation that focuses on a later incident. He does not seem to be able to articulate easily what he has felt very clearly from the moment he first laid eyes on the victim's body that Patrick Kinsley has killed the victim.

In some instances, there is even a radical discrepancy between what people think they do and what people actually do. Chris Argyris and Donald Schön (1974) came up with two models to explain the gap between what we do—generally as a result of rapid cognition processes—and what we say we do: the theory-in-use and the espoused theory, respectively. The theory-in-use is the theory actually employed, whereas the espoused theory consists of the "beliefs, attitudes, and values" that people think guide their behaviors (Argyris, 1993). Argyris and Schön (1974) found that in most cases "there are often fundamental, systematic mismatches between individual's espoused and in-use designs" (Argyris, 1993).

Another phenomenon associated with rapid cognition is that we use critical thinking and other similarly elaborate and long thought processes (System 2 thinking) to justify and rationalize ideas and decisions that were actually made by our rapid cognition system (Kahneman, 2011). We reach a decision intuitively and then we justify it by coming up with a complex explanation that validates the decision generated in the rapid cognition system. For example, when reading a student's essay, we may instantly decide that the essay deserves a B. Then, we will justify our instant decision with our analysis of why the essay is better than an essay that got a C but not as good as an essay that received an A. We may find some mistakes that will support the fact that the essay will not get an A; and we will find some positive aspects in the essay that will endorse our decision not to give the essay a C. In the legal field, the same phenomenon takes place not only with laypeople but also with professionals. Both judges and jurors base their decisions on whether an accused is guilty of a crime or a defendant is liable for damages instantly after encountering the accused or the defendant or reading the file. This is, of course, a subconscious decision that is later justified in terms of legal theories or factual schemes. Incidentally, this phenomenon has led legal realists to claim that judicial cases as well as other legal decisions are "elaborate post hoc realizations for judges to window dress decisions that they have arrived at for personal reasons" (D'Amato, 1984).

Rapid cognition is also responsible for the development of our likes and preferences that range from the actors we like to the cars we prefer. Our preferences and likes also, unconsciously, greatly influence our decisions in areas where we may believe that we reach decisions rationally and analytically such as professional decisions in our careers. Finally, the rapid cognition system is also responsible for the development of our "long-term memory by recording many features of our interactions with the world" (Hogarth, 2003).

Rapid cognition is not a simple thought process. It activates a multitude of neuronal connections. It involves the perception of dozens of stimuli and information, which are analyzed and processed very fast. It also implies acting out and reacting to the conclusions achieved rapidly.

3.3   EMPHASIS ON CRITICAL THINKING SKILLS IN LEGAL AND CRIMINAL JUSTICE EDUCATION

There is a strong emphasis on critical thinking and other analytical thought processes in law schools and criminal justice programs. These thought processes are also essential for personal and professional life. I do not claim that law school and criminal justice programs should do anything to diminish the development of these skills. I do argue that other ways of thinking, including rapid cognition, should also have an important place in the curriculum. Despite the importance of rapid cognition for human thinking, it has a marginal role in the law and criminal justice classrooms.

Given the fact that most of our cognitive processes and most of our decisions in life are generated through rapid cognition rather than System 2 thinking, we should proactively help our students educate their rapid cognition skills alongside critical thinking and other analytical reasoning skills.

Similar to critical thinking, rapid cognition may lead to correct decisions in many cases. In other situations, rapid cognition, just like critical thinking and other thinking processes, can lead to faulty conclusions and decisions. A lawyer may have a feeling that her client is telling her the truth, but he may be lying to her. A police officer may have a hunch that the suspect was involved in a crime, but the officer may be wrong. Also, just like you can teach critical thinking skills and other analytical thought processes to students, you can also help your students educate their rapid cognition processes through a wide range of interventions and strategies (Hogarth, 2003). Like for analytical thought processes and the development of professional skills and substantive knowledge, popular culture also plays an important role in the education of rapid cognition.

3.4 EDUCATING RAPID COGNITION

One of the most important aspects to help students develop effective rapid cognition processes is to practice rapid cognition decisions in authentic or recreated professional settings. You learn how to think intuitively like an experienced criminal lawyer or as an expert parole officer by carrying out the activities that criminal lawyers and parole officers carry out and by immersing yourself in their professional environments. Rapid cognition is developed mainly through tacit learning. Learners pick up the behaviors, attitudes, styles, jargon, and even gestures of those around them. Through exposure to these stimuli, people learn to react like those whom they are in contact with, provided that they are intrinsically motivated and that they do not experience negative effects while exposed to those stimuli (Hogarth, 2003).[1] Learning in the courtroom or police headquarters is ideal, but it is

---

[1]Hogarth (2003) suggests seven guidelines to educate intuition. These are "(i) select and/or create our environments (apprenticeship model); (ii) seek feedback; (iii) impose circuit breakers; (iv) acknowledge emotions; (v) explore connections; (vi) accept conflict in choice; and (vii) make scientific method intuitive."

also possible to learn to improve the effectiveness of rapid cognition by recreating these environments in the classroom.

Learning the discipline is also an essential aspect of rapid cognition. The more and the deeper you know about law or criminal justice the better rapid cognitive decisions you can take. Those who have a vast knowledge, whether developed by conscious learning, tacit learning, or—even better—a combination of both, are the ones who can make the best intuitive decisions. Since the rapid and the analytical thought systems communicate with each other in our brains, what was once the domain of analytical thinking can become the terrain of rapid cognition (Hogarth, 2003). For example, when a police officer drives a police car to chase a suspect for the first time, he or she will have to consciously think analytically about the car chase. When that professional gains more experience, he or she will probably be able to pursue the suspect using System 1 thought processes. If the chase becomes extraordinary, then that police officer may change back to System 2 thinking.

Feedback is an essential aspect of the whole deep-learning process. It is also central in the education of rapid cognition. Obtaining timely feedback about our intuitive decisions helps us improve future rapid cognition decisions. For example, suppose that a parole officer makes an intuitive prediction that a parolee will not jump parole, based only on a quick glance at the parolee's file and a brief observation of the parolee in person. Then, let's assume that the parolee gets intoxicated and breaks the terms of parole. The parole officer receives information (feedback) about the violation of the parole. In the future, when the parole officer gets a new parolee with some similar characteristics and history as that parolee, the parole officer may predict that this time the new parolee will also jump parole. The more feedback one receives about one's rapid cognitive decisions, the more educated the future intuitive decisions will be.

Another factor that is closely connected to feedback is metacognition, which I will fully develop in Chapter 7. Succinctly, metacognition consists of reflecting about one's own learning process through—general and discipline-specific—categories of analysis. For rapid cognitive thought processes, general categories of analysis include the knowledge of how System 1 thinking operates and how human beings make rapid cognitive decisions. Students need to be aware of the existing of both analytical and rapid cognition models. They need to know how we reach intuitive conclusions and how we make decisions based on the information we process rapidly. They need to be aware of "the circumstances in which intuitive errors are probable" and how to prevent them (Kahneman, 2011).

It is also important for an effective metacognitive reflection to be aware of the role that life stories play in rapid cognition. Life stories are fundamental in the way we perceive and evaluate others (Quintana, 2015). Most decisions involving other people, which in many cases may be the majority of the decisions one takes in the professional world, are based on the life stories of those about whom we have to make a decision. In other words, we judge other people by their life stories. When their life stories fit with our own stories, we value them positively. If they do not fit, we instinctively tend to reject them and disvalue them (Schank, 2000). To go back to one of the previous examples, a job interviewer selects a candidate because he or she understands and likes the candidate's life story.

Another aspect of the metacognition process is the need to be aware of biases in mental processes. A bias is a phenomenon that distorts the cognitive process and leads to erroneous conclusions and decisions. A bias that is specific to the rapid cognition process is known as the "sampling of connections between events" (Hogarth, 2003). This bias consists of extrapolating situations, beliefs, and ideas that apply in one context to another context where they do not apply. For example, suppose that an experienced tax attorney who practices in the state of New York is very effective in recognizing fraud by merely looking at a taxpayer's tax return for a few minutes. If that same tax attorney looks at a Canadian tax return and concludes that the Canadian taxpayer committed fraud, the tax attorney's conclusion may be wrong if the fraud offense in Canada differs from the fraud crime in New York.

Another strategy that helps make rapid cognitive thought processes more effectively is a technique used by actors when they prepare for an acting role. While reading a text such as a play or a script for a film or TV show, the actor starts from his or her visceral, instinctive response to the text and "must reject intellectual choices at the beginning of his or her work" (Guskin, 2003). We can adapt this technique to the law and criminal justice classrooms. We can ask students to read a file, such as the presentence report or the deposition of a witness, and tell us their instinctive evaluations about the file. If they try to shift to analytical reasoning, like acting coaches or theater directors, we should help them reject that line of reasoning and help them go back to the rapid cognition mode.

3.5   THE ROLE OF POPULAR CULTURE IN EDUCATING RAPID COGNITION

Popular culture plays an important role in the education of rapid cognition just as it does for the development of analytical thought processes, professional skills, and substantive knowledge.

Popular culture stories, particularly TV shows (sitcoms, reality shows, news programs) and films, privilege the depiction of characters that are intuitive and make rapid cognition decisions. Specifically in the criminal justice and legal practice fields, popular culture also offers multiple opportunities for students to observe lawyers and criminal justice officers take rapid cognition decisions. In some cases, these decisions are effective; and in others they are erroneous. Showing these situations, the ensuing rationalizations, and the results of the actions taken intuitively in class help students discuss and reflect about the rapid cognition process. For example, in *The Silence of the Lambs* (Demme, 1991), agent Clarice Starling glances at a file for a few seconds and takes a quick look at the victim's pictures. When her superior, special agent Jack Crawford, asks her to profile the perpetrator, Starling instantly concludes that he must be white, in his 30s or 40s; he must live in his own house and not an apartment as he needs privacy to carry out the crimes; he must also have physical strength and self-control. Starling also thinks that the perpetrator must be cautious, precise, and impulsive. She also speculates that he will never stop, as he is getting better at his work. Similarly, in *Law and Order: Criminal Intent*'s episode *Tru Love* (Barba, 2006) detectives Mike Logan and Megan Wheeler discuss their gut feelings about the death of Dr. Grant Tyler, a police plastic surgeon. They do so after they have a quick look at the body and his motorcycle and right after they interrogate Keith, his son, his son's teacher, Danielle McCaskin, and other suspects. By having a quick glance at the victim's house, Logan and Wheeler make quick assumptions about Dr. Tyler's social status, his personality, and his last actions before he is killed. They soon realize that Dr. Tyler has had sex with multiple partners, that he has taped his sexual encounters, and that he has kept tapes somewhere in the house. They also interrogate his ex-boss,

Dr. Clayton. While doing so, they briefly scan his office. They look at a picture of a young lady posing at what looks like a college. The detectives instantly know that Dr. Tyler and Dr. Clayton's daughter have had sexual intercourse, which Dr. Clayton strongly objects to. Dr. Clayton takes out a damaged VHS tape out of a drawer, and detective Wheeler instantly realizes that Dr. Tyler has sent him a tape of him having sex with Dr. Clayton's daughter. Then, detectives Logan and Wheeler interrogate Danielle's husband. They soon infer that Danielle and Keith are in love, that they have planned Dr. Tyler's murder together. They also rapidly conclude that they blame Danielle's husband in order to get rid of both Dr. Tyler and Danielle's husband. While interrogating Danielle, the assistant district attorney speculates that Danielle seduced Dr. Tyler to buy his silence about Keith and to frame her husband. After students observe and discuss these situations, you can recreate a similar setting in the classroom for students to face situations where they have to process information fast and take rapid cognition decisions. For example, you can give your students a file with detailed information about cases that were tried in the criminal justice system. Students can read a file for a few minutes and come up with a conclusion about the culpability of the accused. Recreated professional practice situations can be complemented with feedback sessions and metacognitive reflection, which enhance the rapid cognition process. So, after students make their decisions, you can give them feedback about the actual outcome of the cases. This practice is important because

Long before people are able to articulate how they think the system works, they are able to act as though they understand it. Moreover, when people are explicitly instructed to try and learn how the system works—i.e., in deliberate mode—they are not as successful in gaining an understanding as when they interact with the system in more passive, tacit mode. […] We learn by example and by direct experience because there are real limits to the adequacy of verbal instruction. People are ignorant of the things that affect their actions, yet they rarely feel ignorant. (Hogarth, 2003)

Popular culture stories also offer learners the possibility of focusing on obtaining feedback about rapid cognition decisions that people take in films and TV shows, that is to say, learners can observe when characters take a rapid cognitive decision and then see if those decisions were effective or not. If they were not, students can think of and discuss what went wrong and what the individuals who took those decisions need to correct next time they face a similar situation. Continuing with the previous examples, you can show the last scenes of *The Silence of the Lambs* (1991) to see if agent Sterling's rapid profile about Buffalo Bill (Ted Levine) was true. In *Law and Order*'s *Tru Love* episode, just like in real professional life, some of the assumptions the police officers make about Dr. Tyler's crime and the inferences about the role of each suspect are erroneous, and some are correct. Students can discuss what rapid cognition strategies work and what strategies do not work.

3.6 SUMMARY

Rapid cognition, that is to say, the fast processing of stimuli and information that leads to intuitive conclusions and decisions, is pervasive in everyday life, including the criminal justice and legal systems. Despite its importance, it has been relegated to the margins of higher education. Rapid cognition processes can be improved with specific educational interventions. Popular culture offers innumerable possibilities to help students fully develop their rapid cognition skills and to reflect about them.

The next chapter explores the importance of motivation and student engagement for the adoption of a deep-learning approach. It will focus on the role of popular culture texts in promoting intrinsic motivation.

KEYWORDS

- **rapid cognition**
- **educating rapid cognition**
- **critical thinking**
- **cognitive skills**
- **feedback**

CHAPTER 4

Motivation and Student Engagement

Sometimes the wrong train
can get you to the right station.

—The Lunchbox (2014)

ABSTRACT

Intrinsic motivation takes place when students learn because they want to, because they see the importance of learning for their own personal growth. An intrinsically motivated student learns out of curiosity and love for learning, without looking for external rewards. Intrinsic motivation makes students activate the competences, skills, and processes that are necessary for deep learning to occur. Popular culture stories play a powerful role in engaging students and fostering their intrinsic motivation. Popular culture also encourages students to recreate and perform the professional activities of their discipline; and it helps to create an enjoyable and safe environment, which is also conducive to deep learning.

4.1 INTRODUCTION

As discussed earlier in Chapter 2, the deep-learning process requires a connection between new knowledge, embedded in the input story in the form of a problem, question, or situation, and existing knowledge, which makes up our cognitive structure. This connection must activate a series of competences, skills, and processes both at the individual and social levels. Deep learning also requires constant reflection about the learning process and the changes at the individual (cognitive structure) and social levels (professional or academic community).

What is it that makes the learner actually make the connections, activation, reflection, and changes? It cannot be the input story alone. After all, we are exposed to literally hundreds of stories every day (at school, at work, at home, at a bus stop, at the supermarket checkout line) that come from many different sources (teachers, colleagues, bosses, family members, friends, neighbors, television, theater, books, and even complete strangers). But we rarely produce a conceptual change as the result of the exposition to these stories.

This chapter will analyze the factor that makes this process possible: intrinsic motivation. I will begin with a brief examination of the notion of motivation and the two categories of motivation: intrinsic and extrinsic. I will then discuss the factors and conditions that are required for, and that foster, intrinsic motivation, including, the role that popular culture plays in promoting intrinsic motivation. Finally, I will explore some circumstances that deter the occurrence of intrinsic motivation.

4.2 MOTIVATION

In *Erin Brockovich* (2000), directed by Steven Soderbergh, Erin (Julia Roberts) is an unemployed twice-divorced, single mother of three young children. She needs to find a job and, above all, a purpose in life. She manages to land a job as a legal assistant with her former lawyer, Ed Masry (Albert Finney). Erin stumbles upon a real-estate file, which contains medical records. Her instinct tells her that there is something fishy in the file and asks her boss for permission to investigate. Erin becomes passionate about, almost obsessed with, the investigation. She soon realizes that a gas and electric company has contaminated the water in the community adjacent to its compressor plant.

Erin truly enjoys working on this case. She feels elated. She is meticulous and aims at achieving mastery in investigation and legal research. At one point, she realizes that she needs more knowledge on the effects of chromium in the human body. So, she teaches herself advanced notions of chemistry and applies them to her investigations.

Although she faces numerous obstacles in the investigation, she does not get discouraged. She never, ever, gives up. Erin stops going to the firm and devotes full-time to uncover what happened. She needs to be in the community, talking to those affected by the contamination and reading files in the county water board. She needs time. She does not need to be given directions or instructions from a boss. She sets her own goals. Erin wants to get to the bottom of the case. She needs to work freely without directions and control. This does not mean that she only wants to work alone. She seeks out other people who are involved in the case and who can give her helpful advice. She is curious and asks lots of relevant questions.

But her boss does not understand this. He fires her because she is not in the office from 9 to 5 and because she works independently. He takes Erin's initiative and yearning for autonomy as signs of lack of care for her job rather than as relentless passion for rigorous legal work. Ed Masry is only concerned with office discipline. He wants all his employees to follow his orders. He does not care about anything else.

After being fired, Erin is not discouraged. She keeps working hard on the case. She spends tireless hours trying to solve all the puzzles of a very complex environmental law case. Word gets to Ed Masry, who rehires her. And Erin continues to work as passionately as always.

Erin works hard because she wants to help others. She does not seek any rewards or a multimillion-dollar settlement to get a six-figure check. Unlike Ed, who is only interested in his fees, Erin is engaged in the case to improve the lives of the families affected by the pollution of their lands and water. She does not care about recognition. Surely, she is happy when Ed gives her a 2 million dollar check when they win the case. But she is never obsessed with making money for herself.

Motivation is "some kind of internal drive which pushes someone to do things to achieve something" (Harmer, 2001). Motivation determines people to act toward a goal, try hard, and sustain the actions to accomplish the goal. In the deep-learning context, motivation is the force that stimulates the learner to solve the problem, question, or situation embedded in the input story, to activate an existing story, to make connections between the input story and the existing story, to employ higher order cognitive and metacognitive processes, including rapid cognition strategies, to reflect about the learning process, and, more important, to want to change the existing story (cognitive structure) as a consequence of having experienced this whole process. Motivation is what keeps Erin working hard on the case despite her boss's objections, and the powerful defendant's obstacles, and their even more powerful lawyers' deceitful strategies.

There are two types of motivation: extrinsic and intrinsic. Intrinsic motivation, also referred to as engagement, is the genuine desire to do something because you like it, because you see a meaningful connection to your life and personal goals or to a larger purpose. In *La Boum* (Pinoteau, 1980), 13-year-old Vic walks the extra mile to attend *la boum* (the party). Extrinsic motivation is doing something because you have to, because you fear the consequences for not doing it, or because you want to obtain something in exchange for doing it (Quintana, 2017).

4.3　EXTRINSIC MOTIVATION

In the higher education context, extrinsic motivation takes place when learning is geared by a system of rewards and punishments. Students do not try to learn because it is important for their lives and because they are passionate about what they learn. They do so because they are threatened with punishment if they do not or because they are stimulated with rewards if they do. The higher education system is "modeled on 19th century efficiency driven, assembly-line factories, which, in turn, were modeled on the early 19-century prison system that curtailed the body by disciplining the mind" (Duncum, 2009). In this context, rewards come in different forms, usually associated with high grades. But they also include credit for the course, a diploma or degree, a summer internship, a job offer, a scholarship, honors, inclusion in the dean's list, or any other academic prize. Punishment includes a low or failing grade in the course, academic probation, loss of fellowships, failure to secure an internship, or failure to gain a coveted job.

Nowhere is this system of rewards and punishments more tangible than in American, and to a lesser extent Canadian, law schools. It starts with a fierce admissions model which subjects candidates to take a standardized test, the LSAT, which has been criticized for not measuring what it purports to measure, for being discriminatory against minorities, and for being quite arbitrary. The admissions process leaves out hundreds and even thousands of highly capable and motivated students and subjects all candidates to excessive pressure and harmful conditions. From day one, law school students know that their grades, if good enough, will start them on an upward path of endless rewards or, if not good enough, will sink them into a downward spiral of career failures. First-year grades determine who will make the law review and who will get a coveted summer internship in a law firm. This, in turn, will determine who gets a job offer in a prestigious law firm after graduation. This system of rewards and punishments is exacerbated by the introduction of grading-by-the curve evaluation policies. Many law schools, particularly for first-year courses, grade students by the curve, that is, they have a predetermined, low pool of available top grades, a larger pool of mediocre grades, and another small pool of failing grades. No matter how well (or how poorly) students do, only a small percentage will get the top grades.

When the emphasis is on extrinsic factors, students do what they need to get the rewards at the minimum cost for them, that is, they will study without fully committing to deep learning. This excessive institutional emphasis on external motivating factors has resulted in an explosive psychological Molotov cocktail for law school students. Research studies conclusively show that although the majority of students enter law school with internal values and highly intrinsic motivation, before they get to their second year, their intrinsic motivation greatly diminishes or disappears completely; and students are totally disengaged in their second and third years of law school (Sheldon and Krieger, 2004, 2007). Additionally, their general well-being also diminishes; and law school students experience substantially higher rates of depression, anxiety, and other mental health issues than students in other programs and the general population. The number and severity of mental health issues among law school students are only comparable to the emotional distress experienced by psychiatric populations (Dammeyer and Nunez, 1999). These effects of external motivation persist after students have graduated and have entered the legal profession.

Scores of research studies demonstrate that when law school students are exposed to the external rewards and threats of punishment end up experiencing reactance (Sheldon and Krieger, 2007). Student reactance is a phenomenon that occurs when students develop a strong resistance to learning. Once students end their higher education studies and are no longer coerced by grades, they will rarely try to learn academic, university-level materials for the sake of learning (Pollio and Beck, 2000). This is because human beings generally devalue those activities that they are obliged to do and overvalue those that are not allowed to do. "Learning not to learn may become the most lasting lesson of a college education" (Pollio and Beck, 2000).

In other words, if you have an intrinsic interest in something, and you receive external rewards on top of your interest, once those external rewards disappear, the internal motivation disappears, too (Pink, 2009). Suppose you like listening to country music. If I offer you $10 per country song you listen to, after a short while you will lose complete interest in these songs. This is what three psychologists from Stanford University and the University of Michigan found out in the early 1970s. In a famous research experiment, Mark Lepper, David Greene, and Richard Nisbett worked with day-care children who liked to draw. These children spontaneously chose to draw rather than play with other toys at the day care. They visibly enjoyed drawing and felt proud of the pictures they made. The psychologists randomly divided the children into three groups. They took each group to separate rooms and promised one group of children that they would give them a reward after they finished drawing. The researchers did not say anything to the other two groups, which knew nothing about the offer to the first group. After the groups finished drawing, the researchers gave the first group a reward (beautiful blue ribbons with their names inscribed on them). The researchers also gave the second group a reward. This group had not expected the reward, and they were happy to receive it. The psychologists did not give anything to the third group. Again, each group was not aware of the rewards or lack of rewards to the other groups. After two weeks, the first group lost interest in drawing and stopped drawing. The children in this group took up other interests. They played with toys, they played games, they rested, they chatted, but they did not draw anymore. The other two groups, that is to say, the group that got the unexpected reward and the group of children that got nothing, continued drawing and continued enjoying drawing as much as they had done so before the research experiment (Lepper, Greene, and Nisbett, 1973).

Similarly, in *Fading Gigolo* (Allen, 2014), Fioravante is a single middle age man who is successful with women. He likes having sex. And women clearly like having sex with him. Fioravante is creative in bed. He is attentive to the needs of his partners and stops at nothing to give them pleasure. Above all, Fioravante enjoys having sex. When his friend and boss, Murray decides to close down the bookstore where he works, he offers Fioravante a new job: getting laid for money. Murray gets him rich and beautiful women to have sex with and pays him more than he made in the bookstore. Soon, Fioravante loses interest in sex. He falls in love with a traditional Orthodox Jewish woman who does not want to have sex at all. Fioravante feels more comfortable in this sexless relation and abandons his male escort job, which he now perceives as an ordeal.

4.4 INTRINSIC MOTIVATION

Intrinsic motivation, also referred to as engagement, takes place when students learn because they want to, because they see the importance of learning for their own personal growth as human beings. An intrinsically motivated student learns out of curiosity and love for learning, without looking for external rewards.

Humans are naturally curious animals. Children want to learn and will learn if given the freedom to pursue their interests naturally without the constraints of a system of punishments and rewards (Holt, 1995).

> Children are by nature smart, energetic, curious, eager to learn, and good at learning; they do not need to be bribed and bullied to learn; they learn best when they are happy, involved, and interested in what they are doing; they learn least, or not at all, when they are bored, threatened, humiliated, frightened. (Holt, 1995)

This view of learning is supported by neuroscience studies that argue that the search for meaning is innate in human beings and in other animals. For example, rats that were offered a cage-free environment, full of challenging obstacles, objects to play with, and the presence of other rats demonstrated an increase in the size of the cerebral cortex when compared to rats which were isolated in cages with regimented tasks and in a punishment-reward structure similar to the ones used in higher education (Diamond et al., 1964).

So, if children are born with a rich capacity to learn, a passion for learning, and an ardent desire to experiment, how come when they come to law school and university criminal justice programs they do not seem intrinsically motivated to learn? What happens to those innate capacities? The answer is simple. Formal education happens. Years of schooling in a carrot-and-stick system and a society that emphasizes competition slowly kill this innate curiosity. Thus, intrinsic motivation cannot be taken for granted in the law school and university settings. It needs to be created, constantly nurtured, and permanently sustained.

Daniel Pink, a Yale Law School-educated author and business guru, argues that intrinsic motivation requires autonomy, mastery, and purpose. Autonomy implies self-directing one's learning process and having freedom over every element and step of this process. Students need to have autonomy over what they learn, how they learn, when they learn, and with whom they learn (Pink, 2009). Erin Brockovich learned to do legal research for a complex environmental law case alone. She chose when, where, and who to work with. Nobody ever told her that she had to legal research or how to do it. Mastery is the mental attitude that leads you to work hard with determination and perseverance to become better at what you learn, knowing fully well that mastery, like perfection, is an unattainable goal. Erin Brockovich understands the nuances of complex litigation like very few legal professionals. Still, she always feels that she has to keep improving and keeps on learning in a utopian quest toward mastery and perfection. Purpose is the desire to learn something because learning it is connected to a cause that transcends you. You learn because you feel that you are contributing to a larger cause that will bring benefits to others, such as your community, your family, people in need, the arts, the sciences, or society in general. Erin Brokovich conducts her investigation to help the residents of a community who face serious diseases caused by a gas and electric plant's use of dangerous chemicals. For Pink (2009), the achievement of deep learning lies in "our deep-seated desire to direct our own lives, to extend and expand our abilities, and to make a contribution." At law school and university, we need to create the conditions for students to rediscover and unleash their innate motivation to be curious and learn.

4.4.1   FACTORS THAT FOSTER INTRINSIC MOTIVATION: THE INPUT STORY AND POPULAR CULTURE

Popular culture stories are very powerful resources to engage students and foster their intrinsic motivation. Popular culture stories in the classroom act as attention mechanisms, that is to say, devices that foster synchronization of senses with the mind. Students are continually exposed to myriad external stimuli, which compete for their attention even when they are sitting in their higher education classrooms: a fight with their boyfriends or girlfriends the previous night, family responsibilities, friends' recommendations, assignments for other courses, a sports game, gossip, small conversation, and even background noise. The brain can only make one deep-level connection at a time. Multitasking does not exist in the deep-learning process. In other words, students need to focus on the input story alone when grappling with the problem or question embedded in the input story.

There are many factors that determine whether students would choose one issue, if any, over another to give it their deep attention. These factors affecting the capability of stimuli to enter students' inner world are both internal and external. External aspects of the stimulus have to do with the learner's needs, background, experiences, and personal circumstances. They are external because stimulus receptivity does not entirely depend on the stimulus itself but on circumstances and factors that are outside the stimulus, such as those inside the students' minds. In some cases, external aspects of the stimulus are more difficult to control in the law school or criminal justice classroom. As a way of illustration, if a student has broken up a long-term relationship with her fiancé, the student will probably not be very interested in discussing how to do a sentencing report or how to help a victim prepare a victim impact statement. But, in other situations where external stimuli are not very powerful, pressing, or stressful, choosing stimuli that are closer to students' backgrounds and interests is more likely to stimulate students to want to interact with those stimuli than if you choose stimulus that is too detached from students' lives.

Internal aspects of the stimulus have to do with the intrinsic qualities of stimuli. These include stimuli that are enjoyable, interesting, intriguing, beautiful, challenging, and captivating (Bain, 2004). Teachers are more likely to control internal aspects of stimuli, as they can choose the problems, questions, or situations embedded in the input story.

Popular culture texts, when carefully selected to relate to students' backgrounds, are very powerful stimuli. Popular culture texts offer innumerable stories that naturally engage students. Most of these texts are produced by professionals that are experts in the art of telling stories and entertaining. Some of these texts, particularly motion pictures, TV shows, and commercial songs, are works produced with very high budgets and plenty of resources. They offer plots with all possible settings, characters, and situations. These texts speak in a language that learners, who are immersed in a visually—and technologically—oriented culture, are already familiar with. Most students know some of these texts; and they are already motivated to watch, read, or listen to them. Some may even be big fans of these stories, their characters, or the actors who portray them. And some students may already be hooked to these popular culture works. So, employing popular culture texts, such as TV shows, songs, motion pictures, and novels, offers a unique opportunity to motivate the activation of students' existing knowledge structure and their engagement in the deep-learning process. Popular culture stories are intrinsically enjoyable because they permit "to see, in safety, presented through simple words or flat images, what could produce anxiety or dangerous desire. [...] At the other end of the chain, we can see [...] in the 'reproductions' of these easily managed, scaled-down models, a safe and quick way to observe the productive mechanism of human events" (Ubersfeld, 1982).

Additionally, popular culture has a subversive, irrational nature. It breaks rules and exceeds boundaries. It is politically incorrect. It is essentially transgressive (Duncum, 2009). "The characteristic feeling accompanying transgression is one of intense pleasure (at the exceeding of boundaries) and of intense anguish (at the full realization of the force of those boundaries)" (Miller, 1986). This feeling of pleasure clashes with the rationality and formality associated with higher education (Duncum, 2009). So, students that interact with popular culture stories in class experience a transgressive pleasure that motivates them to engage with the problems, situations, and questions embedded in these stories.

What's more, many students view themselves and think about their world through popular culture stories (Giroux and Simon, 1988). They spend hours watching television, listening to music, reading comics, surfing the web, watching commercials, reading books, and reading magazines. Popular culture is part of their daily lives. Popular culture stories, with their plots, themes, characters, settings, conflicts, music, and esthetics, constitute instruments that students already use to think (some quite critically, and other less so) about themselves and their relations to the outside world. So, using these instruments in class creates a familiar environment and a sense of belonging. This, in turn, contributes to the awakening of intrinsic motivation that facilitates students' immersion in the deep-learning process (Lambert et al., 2013).

For these reasons, media texts, particularly segments from films, music clips, and inspirational videos, have long been used to motivate sports athletes. For example, in the 2008–2009 season, Pep Guardiola, then a young coach with no experience whatsoever in any first division club and with only a one-year stint in third division, was appointed to manage Barcelona's senior team—one of the world's powerhouses in soccer. Guardiola's Barcelona, aided by a spectacular Lionel Messi, played brilliant soccer and won every competition they participated in during that season. The most important one was the Champions League. Before the Champions League final in Rome in 2009, Pep Guardiola showed his team a film with scenes from Ridley Scot's *Gladiator* (2000) and scenes with the landmarks of the 2008–2009 season that was culminating with the final match against Manchester United. While the Barcelona team was coming out of the locker room to the pitch, Andrea Bocelli sang *Il Gladiatore* from the film's soundtrack. Barcelona ended up winning the game with an impressive 2–0 victory, which is regarded as one of the best games in soccer history. Guardiola repeated this procedure before other important games in subsequent seasons. In 2010, before another Champions League game, Guardiola showed his players Clint Eastwood's *Invictus* (2009) in its entirety. These popular culture texts gave players extra motivation; they lit fire in them to go out and do their best in the field.

Popular culture texts are increasingly being used in business contexts for the same motivational purposes. There is a long line of research that shows that media texts can be effective instruments to intrinsically motivate people (McNutt & Wright, 1995).

4.4.2   FACTORS THAT FOSTER INTRINSIC MOTIVATION: ENJOYABLE ENVIRONMENT

The creation of an enjoyable teaching and learning environment is a fundamental aspect of intrinsic motivation. Learners learn more profoundly when they enjoy what they do. If they like the input story, students are more likely to enjoy the rest of the learning process. But the input story is not the whole learning environment. This environment is also made up of "faculty-student interaction, the tone instructors set, (…) the course demographics, student-student interaction, and the range of perspectives represented in the course content and materials" (Ambrose et al., 2010). All these factors must also positively contribute to create an enjoyable environment.

Neuroscience confirms the connection between positive emotions and deep learning. There is a very strong connection between the frontal cortex, which is responsible for abstract thinking and other higher order cognitive competences, and the amygdala, which is the emotion hub of the brain (Zull, 2002). "Emotion is probably the most important factor for learning. Our feelings determine the energy with which we begin new challenges and where we will direct that energy. The actions we take are determined by how we feel and how we believe those actions will make us feel" (Zull, 2011).

Teachers' intrinsic motivation to teach a course also contributes to the creation of an enjoyable atmosphere. Teachers' motivation is contagious and passes along to students. "People automatically mimic and synchronize expressions, vocalizations, postures, and movements with others and consequently converge emotionally as a result of the activation and/ or feedback from such mimicry" (Hatfield, Cacioppo, and Rapson, 1992; Mottet and Beebe, 2000). Teachers set the tone and atmosphere of their classes and influence their students' emotions. When teachers are enthusiastic about the class, when they feel passion about the input stories, and when they are genuinely excited about what they are doing, then students will also be enthusiastic, passionate, and excited. This emotional contagion is, generally, an unconscious process, produced through the activation of mirror neurons in our brains (Wicker et al., 2003). Mirror neurons are considered intelligent cells that help us understand and interact with others (Iacoboni, 2005). The same neurons that activate when an individual carries out an activity also activate when the individual observes someone else do that activity (Rizzolatti and Craighero, 2004). We can all relate to that topic or discipline that we never cared about, but when we took a course on that topic or discipline with a particularly passionate teacher we were truly motivated to learn.

There are a number of factors that contribute to increase teacher motivation. One of these factors is the adoption of intensive teaching scheduling formats. Intensive teaching takes place when students take a course over prolonged and uninterrupted blocks of time, instead of the traditional semester-length course schedule formats that range from 60 to 180 minutes one, two, or three days a week. Teachers are more motivated when they teach for long periods of time, particularly if they teach, and students take, only one course at a time. Motivation increases even more for both teachers and students if they can have autonomy over the schedule and can work at their own pace when they feel like it without scheduling constraints (Pink, 2009).

4.4.3   FACTORS THAT FOSTER INTRINSIC MOTIVATION: SAFE ENVIRONMENT

Students also need a stress-free atmosphere to engage in the complex cognitive competences that the process demands. Students learn better and more profoundly when they feel safe and when they do not feel threatened by conscious or unconscious teachers' and other students' attitudes. Students also learn better and more profoundly if they can take risks, try, and make mistakes when the risks and mistakes do not affect their grades and when their attempts and risks are positively valued through feedback and a positive teacher attitude (Bain, 2004). Similarly, we also teach better when we feel safe and relaxed.

Consider the film *Student Seduction* (Svatek, 2003). When chemistry teacher Christie Dawson feels safe and protected in her school, she goes the extra mile to help Josh Gaines, a struggling student. When Josh misinterprets Ms. Dawson's after-hour tutoring for sexual interest in him, he makes a pass at her, but she turns him down. Not used to rejections, Josh is furious. To avenge the rejection, Josh accuses Ms. Dawson of sexually assaulting him. The school principal and her colleagues do not support her while the police investigate the incident. Christie Dawson feels threatened, disvalued, and tense. Consequently, she acts nervously, does not think clearly, neglects to set boundaries with Josh, and makes mistakes that end up worsening her legal situation in the criminal investigation.

A stress-free environment is an environment that emphasizes learners' independence and choice. If students have plenty of options in choosing their goals, in selecting the teaching and learning activities that may help them achieve those goals, and in choosing the means to demonstrate their learning, they feel less stressed and are more likely to enjoy their learning process. In this respect, students can assume and bring to the learning process two different types of goals: performance goals and learning goals. The objective of performance goals is to do better than other students, get better grades, and receive more recognition than others. The aim of learning goals is to understand and master new knowledge (Tagg, 2003). Performance goals invariably lead to surface learning, whereas learning goals may be conducive to deep learning, particularly when students themselves are involved in adopting their own learning goals. Helping students formulate their goals in a stress-free environment is one of the most important aspects for the creation of a safe environment. When students play a role in the determination of their goals, they are more likely to adopt learning goals and discard performance goals. This also fosters intrinsic motivation, as students can relate those goals to their existing interests (Tagg, 2003).

4.4.4 FACTORS THAT FOSTER INTRINSIC MOTIVATION: RECREATION OF THE DISCIPLINE OR PROFESSIONAL WORLD

A motivating learning environment conducive to deep learning also requires classes to shift the focus from teacher teaching to student performance. Students need to perform the activities of their discipline in a frequent and continual fashion, and teachers need to accompany and promote students in their performances (Tagg, 2003). In most law schools and universities, the limelight is on the teacher and not the students. If traditional higher education were a theater play, the teacher would be the playwright, the director, and the lead cast all at the same time. Students would be supporting actors. In some cases, they would only be mere spectators.

Beautiful Music (Trank, 2005) recounts the story of Devorah Schramm, a dedicated and passionate music teacher in Israel, and Rasha Hamid, one of her most accomplished students. Rasha is a blind and fragile girl in the autism spectrum, who was abandoned by her biological parents and suffered the cruelty of the Middle East conflict first-handedly. When she first came to study with Devorah, Rasha was quiet, introspective, and distrustful of most people. After years of studying with Devorah, Rasha grew to love music. She developed pianistic skills and a wonderful sense of playing music that are rarely seen in even the most prestigious professional musicians. Rasha now shines in concerts in front of large audiences—something unimaginable for someone in the autism spectrum. Rasha also became a very talented music composer. Her musical compositions are colorful, romantic, and harmonious. Above all, she learned to communicate with the outside world by sharing her passion for music. Devorah explains her teaching approach, which consists of helping Rasha immerse in authentic activities in the field of music, as follows:

> [Rasha played the piano for hours every day.] I just jumped in there and participated in her world. And when I could add something from my professional experience—something to help her in her world, I would jump in and do it. Meanwhile, I was assessing her all the time. I was constantly assessing and seeing what I could do.

Most law school and criminal justice classes at both the undergraduate and graduate levels focus, at best, on few selected aspects of the legal and criminal justice professions, respectively, and, at worse, on none. Law schools in North America tend to focus on only some aspects of the work of appellate lawyers. The works of trial lawyers occupy a marginal role, often relegated to clinical courses and moot court competitions. But the work of a lawyer exceeds these activities. Lawyers interview clients, give advice, write contracts, produce legal opinions, participate in arbitration, mediate, make presentations to partners and to corporate clients, negotiate fees, converse with other lawyers, seek advice, hire associates, evaluate associates, manage a firm, buy legal software, talk to the press, and attend conferences, among many other activities. Law schools ignore most of these activities. Similarly, criminal justice programs tend to focus on the explanation of topics through lecture and textbooks (undergraduate level) and the discussion of journal articles (graduate level). The criminal justice professional seldom, if ever, does this. The professional supervises parolees, conducts risk factor assessments, arrests suspects, interrogates witnesses, investigates crimes, converses with other criminal justice professionals, assists crime victims, attends conferences, talks to the press, and reformulates policy, among many other issues. None of these activities have room in the traditional university classroom.

If students can engage in most or all of these activities, either in authentic settings or in recreated activities in the classroom, including those activities that are not traditionally considered strictly academic, such as talking to the press or hiring associates, they will be more motivated to engage in the deep-learning process (Perkins, 2009). Students are more motivated when they can experience the whole picture of the discipline and not just an artificially selected fraction.

4.4.5 FACTORS THAT FOSTER THE CREATION OF A MOTIVATING ENVIRONMENT: TEACHERS' EXPECTATIONS

Teachers' expectations about their students' potential to do well in their classes and in future academic and professional endeavors greatly influence students' motivation both positively and negatively. If teachers genuinely expect great things from their students, students will feel motivated to work hard and learn deeply (Bain, 2012).

In a very well-known research experiment, two researchers—a psychology professor at Harvard University and a grade school principal—approached several elementary teachers and told them that their students had taken a rigorous and difficult standardized test. They also told them that some students had done very well and that they had a lot of potential for intellectual performance. The test did not exist, so no student had taken it. The researchers had randomly selected the names of the students that were identified as the highest achievers in the—nonexistent—test (Rosenthal and Jacobson, 1965). Rosenthal and Jacobson followed these students' performances. All these students did very well. They had the highest marks in the courses. Teachers' expectations acted like self-fulfilling prophecies. The teachers had very high expectations of these students, which motivated them to perform well. This experiment was replicated hundreds of times (Rosenthal and Rabin, 1978). The results consistently show that the effects of teachers' expectations have an impact on students for a long time, even years after they finish the course (Smith, Jussim, and Eccles, 1999).

Devorah Schramm has great expectations of all students. She has many students who, like Rasha, have what others refer to as—learning and physical—disabilities. She sincerely expects the best from every student and acts accordingly, offering every single student the best possible environment to develop their potential.

> As a teacher, when I look at a student I look at their potential. I look at them as a human being with a potential to develop. So, when I have a student that has what they call a disability, I look at them a bit different and say 'OK, I'll work with you as you are, and I am not just going to put you on the forum and make you as society wants you to be. You are all right as you are; and I want to take you as you are and give you some happiness and share with you what I love. And I am not going to pity you. I'm going to give to you.' (Beautiful Music, 2005)

4.4.6 FACTORS THAT PREVENT THE CREATION OF A MOTIVATING ENVIRONMENT

Apart from a system of rewards and punishments and teachers' negative expectations of their students, which as discussed earlier, conduce to surface learning, there are other several factors that prevent the creation of an intrinsically motivating environment. One of these factors is the creation of a stressful classroom atmosphere. A stressed environment produces too much adrenaline, which ends up obstructing the functions of the frontal cortex and in extreme cases even reducing the size of the cerebral cortex (Meaney et al., 1988). A very heavy workload which students perceive as unmanageable (Prosser and Trigwell, 1999) generates a stressed environment. Similarly, inflexible attitudes and a too distant teacher-student relation, such as the one personified by Professor Kingsfield (John Houseman) in James Bridges's 1973 film *The Paper Chase*, also produce a stressful atmosphere.

Two other factors that generate a negative environment are stereotyping and discrimination (Quintana, 2017). Although overt discrimination and stereotyping are rarer today than a few decades ago, subtler forms of stereotyping, such as stereotype threat and discrimination, are common in some higher education institutions. Stereotype threat is a phenomenon that takes place when people are reminded of their gender or race when these are associated with culturally shared stereotypes suggesting negative academic performance. In those cases, the performance of such students on certain tasks is more likely to conform to the stereotype (Handelsman, Miller, and Pfund, 2007). Steele and Aronson (1995) introduced this concept when they noticed that African American undergraduate students did worse than white students when they were reminded of their race just before completing an academic task. When there was no emphasis on race they did as well or even better than white students. Similar results occurred with other minority groups (Nguyen and Ryan, 2008). For example, Asian female students were given a questionnaire before doing a math assignment. Some students received a questionnaire that focused on Asian ethnicity; other students received a questionnaire that focused on gender; a third group of students received a questionnaire that focused on neither. In the United States, it is a popular stereotype that Asian students are good at math. A similarly popular stereotype is that males are better than females in math. Results show that those students who were reminded of their Asian background performed better than the other groups. Students who received the questionnaire that focused on gender performed the worst (Shih, Pittinsky and Ambady, 1999). A similar phenomenon takes place when students work in small groups, whether in class or outside class. If there is only one member of a minority, such as an African American or an Asian student, in an otherwise all-white group, that minority student will constantly be reminded of his or her race, which will have the same consequences as in the studies where students were reminded of their ethnicity through a questionnaire. The same occurs if there is only one female student in an all-male group (Handelsman, Miller, and Pfund, 2007).

Our attitudes toward race, gender, and other social factors work on two planes: the conscious and the unconscious. The conscious plane includes our explicit values, which guide our intentional behaviors. The unconscious plane includes the immediate associations that these factors generate in our brains (Gladwell, 2005). For example, research shows that many Americans, whether white, black, brown, or any other color, unconsciously associate the notions of evil and bad with African American and good and wonderful with European American (Gladwell, 2005). The unconscious plane guides our unintentional behaviors. Because of the unconscious nature of this phenomenon, we are unaware of these associations and the instant behaviors that they trigger. For example, I once observed a colleague (a well-meaning person with a very open attitude toward diversity) teaching a criminology course in a criminal justice program. She has asked my help because many of her students were not engaged in the class and were turning in acceptable but not stellar works. She was not concerned with grades. Students were getting decent grades because they studied and complied with all formal requirements of the course. But she noticed that there was a level of apathy about some students that she found quite discomforting. So, I attended several of her classes over a semester.

Like in most universities, students were free to sit wherever they pleased in her class. Most Latino students chose—probably unconsciously—to sit in the left rows, whereas most white American students sat in the center rows. The front right rows were occupied mostly by African American students; and international students, mostly from Asia and the Middle East, sat in the back right rows. Of course, there were exceptions; and some students sat with students of other races. After a month and a half into the semester, I came to realize that whenever my colleague explained an elaborate criminological theory, she invariably looked at the middle row that was full of white American students. Whenever she gave an example of a crime, particularly a crime usually associated with lower classes, she looked at either her left or right. When she talked about housekeeping issues, such as deadlines, assignments, evaluation criteria for tests and papers, her eyes panned the classroom, spending equal time with all rows.

My colleague and I met in her office, as she wanted to see if I could come up with some ideas to help students engage in her class. I commented what I had observed about the direction of her looks in class. She was shocked and assured me that she was not aware of this. She made a point of changing this pattern. After a few classes in which she consciously managed to look at all students while discussing theories and types of crimes, students, particularly minority students who had been thus far unengaged, became more motivated in class. They participated more, asked questions, contributed examples, and improved the quality of their assignments.

In *The Blue Lagoon* (Kleiser, 1980), when Paddy discusses activities usually associated with males, such as hunting, fishing, and building, he—unconsciously—looks at Richard—never at Emmeline. Paddy looks at her when he talks about eating, decorating, or other activities associated with females. When he discusses prohibitions and activities that are regarded as gender neutral, he looks at both Emmeline and Richard.

Another factor that hinders the creation of a safe environment is a relatively new and subtle discriminatory phenomenon that occurs in some higher education institutions across North America. In the name of multiculturalism, some universities favor one single minority group over all other minority groups through often well-intentioned diversity initiatives, which tend to grant privileges to a minority group that has been traditionally considered to have been oppressed by the dominant majority group in the geographical area where the university is located. In many cases, the oppression has disappeared or substantially diminished, at least when compared to the oppression and disadvantaged conditions currently experienced by other minority groups. Members of the favored minority group are seen as "sainted victims" and are perceived as good regardless of historical facts and actual individual behaviors. At the same time, the needs of other minority groups are ignored (Younkins, 2007). Minority groups that have been equally or—in some cases even more badly—repressed both in the past and in the present feel doubly victimized by this policy. In many cases, this attitude is carried over to the classroom where readings, content, examples, and projects revolve around the favored minority group and/or the majority group. These actions exacerbate the problems of neglected minority students.

Even in relaxed, enjoyable, nondiscriminatory, and nonstereotyping learning environments, challenging and changing longstanding beliefs may cause learners to experience emotional trauma (Bain, 2004). So, a safe classroom environment needs to make sure that students receive the support which they need as they enter a new academic or professional community.

4.5　SUMMARY

Motivation is the internal drive that makes people do things to accomplish goals. There are two types of motivation extrinsic and intrinsic. In the learning context, extrinsic motivation occurs when learning is encouraged by potential rewards for those who work hard and threatened with punishments for those who do not apply themselves. These rewards and punishments revolve around grades. Years of exposure to extrinsic motivation may give rise to student reactance, that is to say, students may develop a strong resistance to pursuing academic endeavors in their professional lives. Intrinsic motivation comes from within the students. They learn because they recognize the importance of learning and because they find pleasure in learning.

There are several factors that foster intrinsic motivation in the law school and university classrooms. Popular culture texts tend to engage students, as they act as attention mechanisms that students find easy to relate to. Another factor that contributes to generate intrinsic motivation is the creation of an enjoyable and safe environment. One of the most powerful ways to generate intrinsic motivation is by helping students engage in the whole world of the legal and criminal justice professions. Students are motivated when they can actively participate in all aspects of the discipline through authentic—or recreated—professional performances and activities.

Factors that prevent the creation of an intrinsically motivating environment include the creation of a stressful classroom atmosphere, discrimination, and stereotyping, whether these are done in an overt or subtle fashion.

In the next chapter, I will explore the relation between stories and academic disciplines, focusing on the stories that law and criminal justice narrate inside and outside the courtroom. I will also discuss the use of popular culture as an alternative to print materials in law school and criminal justice programs.

KEYWORDS

- **motivation**
- **intrinsic motivation**
- **extrinsic motivation**
- **motivating environment**
- **learning environment**
- **teacher's expectations**

CHAPTER 5

Academic Disciplines and Storytelling: Teaching Law with Popular Culture Stories

Story is a metaphor for life.

—Robert McKee (1997)

ABSTRACT

Academic disciplines tell stories. Law tells the story that it is possible to regulate human conduct through laws, which judges can enforce objectively to restore justice when there has been a breach of the law. Criminal justice tells the stories of police, the courts, and prisons. These stories have a structure that resembles the structure of stories found in popular culture. The great number of popular culture stories on law and criminal justice has given rise to the field of law and popular culture, which is concerned with the mutual influence that each exercises over the other. However, popular culture texts are not often used as sources for the study of law or criminal justice. Teaching law and criminal justice with stories from popular culture offers students the possibility of examining substantive aspects of the legal and criminal justice disciplines while at the same time they help them develop the skills and competences that are essential for legal and criminal justice professionals.

5.1 INTRODUCTION

Higher education institutions have dissected academic disciplines "into tiny, specialized fragments" (Hedges, 2009) and have given them an elitist vocabulary that made them impenetrable for any outsider, including students and other highly educated academics (Hedges, 2009). However, at their core, academic disciplines tell simple—and at the same time grandiose—stories about most essential aspects of human life. Popular culture also tells stories about these same essential aspects with a narrative structure that is not altogether different from the structure of disciplinary stories.

This chapter begins with an analysis of the stories that academic disciplines tell. Then, I will focus on the stories that law and criminal justice narrate both inside and outside the courtroom. I will analyze the existing compatibility between legal and criminal justice stories and stories told in popular culture. Then, I will explore the law and popular culture field, focusing on its shortcomings with respect to teaching and student learning. Finally, the chapter considers the use of popular culture as an alternative to casebooks and legal and criminal justice textbooks. It includes many concrete examples of how to use popular culture texts in order to foster discussion aimed to both help students discover and construct new knowledge about law and criminal justice and to develop skills and competences that are essential for the legal and criminal justice professionals.

5.2   ACADEMIC DISCIPLINES AND STORIES

The Accused (Kaplan, 1988) tells the story of a victim of a sexual assault and a prosecutor who does not understand the victim's story at first. Sarah Tobias is gang raped in a bar full of people who cheer and clap to incite the rapists. Sarah, a low-class, uneducated young woman with an expunged criminal record and a promiscuous sexual life, tells Kathryn Murphy, assistant deputy attorney, her story. Kathryn discusses Sarah's story with her boss and a colleague. After tying up some loose ends, Kathryn prepares quite hard for the bail hearing. She works on the story to adapt it to use it in court.

In a difficult bail hearing, the judge releases the accused on bail. Then, Kathryn works on the story to tell it to the defense attorneys in a plea bargain. Sarah learns about the plea bargain through a story she watches on television. Although her rapists will do prison time, they will not go to trial because the prosecution does not believe that she is a strong witness. Sarah desperately wants to tell her story in court. So, Kathryn agrees to prosecute those who cheered, yelled, and clapped for criminal solicitation. Knowing that she will need to improve Sarah's story for the trial, Kathryn continues to work hard in refining the legal principles applicable to the case. She also keeps investigating, talking to key witnesses, and uncovering new evidence. Meanwhile, the defense attorneys also work on their stories. They interrogate witnesses, they gather evidence, and they obtain data about the victim. They tell their stories to the press and in court. Sarah finally gets to tell her story in court, which helps put the accused behind bars and to feel redeemed. The film narrates all the multiple legal and criminal justice stories related to the rape and its solicitation. And it does so by respecting the logic, language, structure, and narrative style of both legal and film stories.

Every discipline tells a story, a foundational story that glues all members of the discipline together (Quintana and Hermida, 2019). Sociology tells the story of human social behavior. In this story, sociologists narrate the origin and development of social institutions and organizations. They tell this story by focusing on the analysis of social class, religion, work, gender, and social stratification, among other themes. Biology tells the story of life and living organisms. Biologists focus their story on cells, genes, and evolution. Human beings, animals, and plants are all protagonists of this story. History tells the story of human past. It narrates historical events. It does so by focusing on texts and other sources that reconstruct lives, cultures, and events. Psychoanalysis tells the story of the human mind through a fascinating journey into the unconscious, which takes the protagonists to navigate their own dreams, fears, and fantasies. Protagonists engage in telling stories by spontaneously saying the first things that come into their minds no matter how painful, irrational, or illogical they might sound. This permits the spectator to penetrate their childhood traumas, desires, and repressed thoughts and emotions. Criminology tells the story of crime. It deals with the causes, nature, extent, control, and prevention of criminal behavior, as well as society's reaction and response to crime. Similarly, criminal justice tells the story of the system that deals with crime and each of its agents and organs, such as police, the courts, and prisons. Law is no exception. It tells the story of the regulation of human behavior through a system of rules and principles that officials enforce through punitive and privative sanctions.

These stories are sacred. The members of the disciplines believe these stories almost as a matter of faith, without questioning their authenticity or core elements. The stories of academic disciplines contain myths that intend to explain what the discipline does and can achieve. Thus, for example, sociology created the myth that it can explain all social phenomena through its method and that it can influence social policy. The myth in the biology story is that evolution can account for the emergence and development of all forms of life. History created the myth that human beings can get rid of present preconceptions and that they can understand their past without employing present worldview lenses. Criminology's myth is that it can explain why people commit crimes. Criminal justice perpetuated the myth that it can protect individuals and society, while at the same time it can control and prevent crime with equity and fairness. Law, particularly in the common law world, created the myth of the rule of law that separates the laws from the people (and the ruling class) that enacted them, as if the law had a life of its own and as if respecting the law were not the same as obeying those who created it (Hermida, 2018). Another aspect of this myth is that given the right resources and circumstances, a good lawyer can swing a verdict any way he or she wants in court without altering or damaging the public's image of the legal system. Popular culture, with its multiple stories about law and lawyers, help perpetuate this myth.

Apart from the general, foundational, story of the discipline, each discipline also tells a multitude of smaller stories that, in turn, contribute to the larger disciplinary story. To continue with the examples, sociology tells stories about particular social institutions, discrimination of certain groups, and the prevalence of deviance in a certain community. Biology tells stories about the evolution of the human brain, the mechanical and biochemical processes of animals, and the interaction between specific organisms and their environment. History tells stories about long-forgotten civilizations, historical figures, wars, and revolutions. Criminology tells stories about victims of crimes, perpetrators of crime, domestic violence, crime prevention, and juvenile delinquency. Similarly, criminal justice tells stories about police officers, prosecutors, judges, criminal defense attorneys, parole and probation officers, and prison wardens. Law tells stories about individuals who committed crimes, corporations that failed to comply with government regulations, couples who divorce, and rich people who leave their fortune to their lovers and mistresses.

5.3 STORYTELLING AND LAW AND CRIMINAL JUSTICE

There are many layers of storytelling in law as well as in criminal justice told through a myriad of oral and written narratives (Sutherland, 2011). Suspects and witnesses tell stories to the police. The police tell stories to prosecutors. Clients tell stories to their lawyers. For example, a client may tell her lawyer that her husband abused her and that she had to kill him to preserve her life. Another client may tell his lawyer that he was at the murder scene, but he did not rape and kill the victim. Another client may tell her lawyer that she had to forge a check in order to feed her children. Then, lawyers tell these stories to their partners. Lawyers tell stories when examining and cross-examining witnesses, as the "story is the most persuasive technique known" (MacArthy, 2007). Lawyers also tell stories to judges and jurors.

The most important source of law in the common law tradition is the case (judicial decision)[1]. The case is a narrative of facts carefully selected by the judge that tells a story of a dispute involving, at least, two people. The case also includes a selection and analysis of the relevant law applicable to those facts also crafted in narrative form. Finally, the case includes a conclusion where the judge resolves the dispute according to whom he or she thinks is right.

Many of the landmark cases tell fundamental stories of human life. They revolve around issues that are of central importance to people such as life and death, the origins of life, the end of human life, the killing of human beings, the right to defend oneself and others, religion freedoms, and other essential human rights. In order to decide these cases, judges delve into philosophical questions that may exceed the traditional boundaries of the legal discipline. In many instances, judges narrate these stories in intensely dramatic terms. For example, R. v. Dudley and Stephens, the 1884 leading case from the United Kingdom that established that necessity is not a defense to murder, vividly recounts the adventures of shipwrecked crew that commits cannibalism in order to survive[2].

---

[1]In civil law, both the Codes and the work of authors that interpret the codes and other legislation assume the role of telling the main stories.
[2]On July 5, 1884, the prisoners, Thomas Dudley and Edward Stephens, with one Brooks, all able-bodied English seamen, and the deceased also an English boy, between 17 and 18 years of age, the crew of an English yacht, a registered English vessel, were cast away in a storm on the high seas 1600 miles from

Almost all cases, even those that are not considered landmarks, are in essence stories about human life, conflict, and misery. Although criminal law is probably the area of law that narrates the most interesting stories, every other legal area—from property law to tax law—also tells stories (Hermida, 2018). Even legal documents that never make their way to the courts tell stories. For example, contracts tell the stories of buyers and sellers acquiring goods and services. Wills tell stories of unfaithful husbands, ungrateful children, or materialistic widows. Tax returns tell stories of people and corporations earning income through their professions and businesses and a greedy government taking a cut of those earnings.

Similarly, criminal justice reports, documents, and policies are also replete with stories. For example, the risk assessment report prepared by a parole office in the preparation of a parole hearing tells the story of the offender's criminal and social history, the role of alcohol or drugs in the offender's criminal behavior, the offender's attitude of indifference to the criminal behavior, and its impact on the victim. It may also tell the story of violence or abuse of family members, participation in treatment programs, and mental health status. It also tells the story of the offender's institutional

---

the Cape of Good Hope, and were compelled to put into an open boat belonging to the said yacht. That in this boat they had no supply of water and no supply of food, except two 1 lb. tins of turnips, and for 3 days they had nothing else to subsist upon. That on the fourth day they caught a small turtle, upon which they subsisted for a few days, and this was the only food they had up to the twentieth day when the act now in question was committed. That on the twelfth day the turtle was entirely consumed, and for the next 8 days they had nothing to eat. That they had no fresh water, except such rain as they from time to time caught in their oilskin capes. That the boat was drifting on the ocean, and was probably more than 1000 miles away from land. That on the eighteenth day, when they had been 7 days without food and five without water, the prisoners spoke to Brooks as to what should be done if no succor came, and suggested that someone should be sacrificed to save the rest, but Brooks dissented, and the boy, to whom they were understood to refer, was not consulted. That on the July, 24, the day before the act now in question, the prisoner Dudley proposed to Stephens and Brooks that lots should be cast who should be put to death to save the rest, but Brooks refused consent, and it was not put to the boy, and in point of fact there was no drawing of lots. That on that day the prisoners spoke of their having families, and suggested it would be better to kill the boy that their lives should be saved, and Dudley proposed that if there was no vessel in sight by the morrow morning the boy should be killed. That next day, the July, 25, no vessel appearing, Dudley told Brooks that he had better go and have a sleep, and made signs to Stephens and Brooks that the boy had better be killed. The prisoner Stephens agreed to the act, but Brooks dissented from it. That the boy was then lying at the bottom of the boat quite helpless, and extremely weakened by famine and by drinking sea water, and unable to make any resistance, nor did he ever assent to his being killed. The prisoner Dudley offered a prayer asking forgiveness for them all if either of them should be tempted to commit a rash act, and that their souls might be saved. That Dudley, with the assent of Stephens, went to the boy, and telling him that his time was come, put a knife into his throat and killed him then and there; that the three men fed upon the body and blood of the boy for 4 days; that on the fourth day after the act had been committed the boat was picked up by a passing vessel, and the prisoners were rescued, still alive, but in the lowest state of prostration..."

behavior or the offender's behavior during temporary absences, the release plan, evidence of change, and efforts aimed at mitigating the risk factors.

5.4 COMPATIBILITY BETWEEN THE STRUCTURE OF LEGAL AND CRIMINAL JUSTICE STORIES AND STORIES IN POPULAR CULTURE

The stories that clients, police officers, prosecutors, lawyers, and other agents involved in the legal and criminal justice systems tell share the same elements and a similar narrative structure as popular culture texts—albeit in a messier and more disorganized way, particularly when these stories are told outside a court of justice. Lawyers usually clean up these stories when they tell them to jurors, judges, or other lawyers.

> In courtroom persuasion, this process requires that every aspect of a lawyer's presentation directly advances the theory and themes of the case. A lawyer may leave a particularly brutal and entertaining piece of cross-examination on the cutting-room floor, if he (sic) knows the line of questioning […] would not further the theory of the defense (Passon, 2010).

Recognizing the importance of the effects of well told stories in the public opinion and its impact on a court case, in *Chicago*, Marshall, 2002, Billy Flint liberally and artfully edits Roxie Hart's story for the media, particularly for the yellow press. In a press conference, Roxie becomes Flint's dummy, and Flint literally speaks for her.

As discussed in Chapter 2, the structure of popular culture texts in North America generally includes a setup, a conflict, and the resolution of the conflict.[3] During the setup, the author or director introduces the characters, the time, the environment, the location, and the characters' backgrounds, circumstances, conditions, statuses, and positions. The conflict, usually the lengthiest part of the story, is the problem, generally framed in light

---

[3]Because of the global influence of the Hollywood entertainment industry, these stories reach a very large population practically all over the world. However, the structure of both popular culture stories and the stories told in the legal and criminal justice fields outside North America and some parts of Western Europe follow a different structure. North American stories (in both the popular culture and the legal and criminal justice fields) "only take place if [they are] connected to a central conflict" which reflects a predominant American worldview that is based on a presumption of hostility that does not exist in other parts of the world (Ruiz, 1995). Stories told outside North America and parts of Western Europe do not necessarily revolve around a central conflict where protagonists want to achieve something and antagonists obstruct (Malla, 2013).

of opposition of internal or external forces that the characters face. The purpose of the conflict is to arouse readers', listeners', or viewers' interest in the story. Characters suffer transformations as a result of the events that they experience. The conflict may have a: (1) rising action, when events build up until the turning point (the climax), (2) a climax that signals a change in the main characters' situation, and (3) the falling action, when the conflict untangles. Finally, the resolution of the story contains the solution to the problem and the conclusion of the main events.

Legal and criminal justice stories in North America, including stories that defense lawyers tell in court and reported appellate decisions where judges tell their own version of these stories, narrate events in a way that resembles stories told in popular culture texts. For example, judicial cases begin with a detailed account of the facts, which is similar to the setup of popular culture texts. Facts are not "an objective account of the relevant evidence, but rather a narrative carefully crafted to support a particular legal resolution" (Sutherland, 2013). In addition to the facts, the case includes a conflict of a legal nature with the judges' analysis. Finally, the legal decision contains the legal resolution of the story, that is to say, whether the person is guilty of a crime, whether he or she is liable for damages, or whether he or she can have her marriage annulled, among many possibilities.

Legal and criminal justice stories used in professional practice also share many of the elements of popular culture stories: a solid story that is integrated to advance the theory of the case or the plot, respectively, compelling characters who the judge and jurors or the audience can relate to in some meaningful way, and emotionally evocative images (Passon, 2010).

5.5   THE LAW AND POPULAR CULTURE FIELD

This compatibility between stories told in legal and criminal justice practice and popular culture has led to the burgeoning development of popular culture texts with a legal or criminal justice topic, which gave rise to a genre known as popular legal culture.[4] These works include a wide array

---

[4]There are literally thousands of films, TV shows, plays, radio shows, novels, short stories, and songs with legal and criminal justice topics. They go back to the birth of popular culture. For example, radio produced shows such as Crime Does Not Pay, a late 1940's show that aired on MGM New York and Crime Classics an early 1950's CBS show that narrated famous crimes. The list of films is virtually infinite. It includes classics such as To Kill a Mockingbird, The Verdict, The Scottsboro Boy, Anatomy

of legal topics both outside the criminal justice arena such as civil litigation, divorce, and the lives of lawyers, and within the criminal justice field such as criminal trials, police investigation, detective work, and prison life. Some of these texts are based on actual court transcripts, statements, or police investigations. Others are entirely fictional products.

Given the popularity of shows and books with a legal topic, it is no surprise that academics have focused on the analysis of popular culture texts that deal with legal issues. In the last two decades and a half, legal scholars have been publishing books and articles in prestigious law reviews and other publications about popular culture with a legal theme. Many conferences are organized every year around popular culture and the law that attract top and emerging legal scholars. Many law schools as well as undergraduate and graduate university law programs now offer courses on law and popular culture. All this has recently given rise to a new field known as law and popular culture.

The object of this field of study is the popular culture texts with a focus on law, lawyers, and the legal system. It deals with both the role law plays in popular culture and the role popular culture plays in law. It also examines the images of lawyers and the legal system in popular culture texts. In addition, it analyzes whether, and to what extent, popular culture can influence jurors and legal professionals. Another topic that is recurrent in the field is the examination of whether the image of lawyers and the legal system portrayed in popular culture is accurate. For these purposes, law and popular culture texts analyze films, TV shows, and novels on law and try to outline their answers from these analyses.

There are two issues that are conspicuously absent from the law and popular culture field. The first one, which I will discuss in Chapter 6, is a lack of a solid scholarship on the analysis of the conventions of legal popular culture in the law school and law-related university curricula. Authors do not dissect the particular language and conventions of films and other popular media texts dealing with law and criminal justice. In Elkins' terms: "much of this scholarly work on law and popular culture turns out to have little value […] in helping students 'read' films and put them to use as part of their legal education" (Elkins, 2007).

---

of a *Murder*, *12 Angry Men*, *Dead Man Walking*, *Class Action*, and *Kramer versus Kramer*. The list of TV shows is equally endless—from *Perry Mason* to *Law and Order* and its countless spin-offs. Whenever a new medium arose, it soon embraced legal topics. A quick search on YouTube results in millions of videos produced by individuals from all over the world that narrate stories on law and criminal justice events.

The second issue that is not usually present in law and popular culture texts (which I will discuss in the remaining of this chapter) is the use of popular culture works as primary sources for law teaching. Very few authors examine the benefits of using popular culture texts for studying law instead of the traditional casebooks focused on edited appellate court decisions or the legal and criminal justice textbooks widely used in the university classroom.

5.6   TEACHING WITH POPULAR CULTURE STORIES

Teaching with stories from popular culture offers an alternative to reported cases and law and criminal justice textbooks. There are several reasons why stories, especially those told in popular legal culture, should occupy a central spot in the classroom.

Popular culture texts generally offer stories that are narrated as they occur in real life, that is to say, they have not been cleaned up by lawyers, judges, casebook authors, or law professors. Students, through class discussions and activities, can do the legal analysis. In this sense, they offer an additional advantage over traditional judicial decisions and other legal texts published on casebooks and textbooks that are already processed and devoid of nonlegal issues.

There are no empirical studies that suggest that teaching with print-based cases is the best or most effective way for students to learn law, criminal justice, or any other academic or professional discipline. Neither is there evidence that teaching law nor criminal justice from lectures based on textbooks helps students learn deeply. Furthermore, there are no data that demonstrate that teaching with cases or textbook leads to better results than when students learn with popular culture stories and other media texts.

5.7   EXAMPLES OF POPULAR CULTURE LAW AND CRIMINAL JUSTICE AS TEACHING SOURCES

Popular culture can serve as sources for students to analyze cases, situations, and problems from legal and criminal justice perspectives. There are several possibilities to work with popular culture texts as sources in the classroom. One activity that has been tried in the law school classroom and that has been reported in the teaching and learning literature is the analysis of scenes from popular TV shows and commercial motion pictures whose main theme is not a legal or police one, but which offer situations that may have legal or criminal justice consequences and which may be analyzed from legal and criminal justice perspectives.

As a way of illustration, when you want your students to analyze the crime of stalking, you can show some scenes from several films and TV shows that depict situations that constitute the crime of stalking as well as situations that resemble the crime but that lack some elements of the offence. For example, in *Family*'s episode entitled *Someone's Watching* (1977, S2 E 15), Nancy Lawrence, an attractive law school student and single mother, feels that someone is following her, observing what she does all the time. She receives unexpected presents for herself and for her baby from an overzealous secret admirer. If she needs something, whether it is herbs for a meal or notes for her law school class she has missed, he will have them delivered to her. If he does not like what Nancy wears, he gives her something more conservative to wear. Nancy gets terrified. She fears for her life and her baby's life. She goes to the police with her dad, an experienced attorney, and her mother. But the police will not do anything, which makes Nancy feel even more vulnerable. Students can discuss whether Nancy's secret admirer committed the crime of stalking in California.[5] Students can also discuss whether his actions would constitute stalking in other North American jurisdictions that do not follow the California model such as New York or Canada (Gregson, 1998). This episode lends itself for expanding strictly legal discussions and introducing criminological considerations. For example, students can learn about the criminological categories of stalkers.[6] Students can debate

---

[5]California Penal Code 646.9.

[6]The traditional classification of stalkers includes: (1) simple obsession, (2) love obsession, and (3) erotomania. Simple obsession stalking is usually an extension of a previous pattern of domestic violence and psychological abuse. Stalkers in this category try to re-establish a relationship with their former spouses or partners. When victims attempt to remove themselves from such controlling situations, stalkers often feel that their power and self-worth have been taken from them. In such cases, stalkers will often take drastic steps to restore personal self-esteem. It is when stalkers reach this desperate level that they may feel they have nothing to lose and become most volatile. Love obsession stalkers seek to establish a personal relationship with the object of their obsession—contrary to the wishes of their victims. Love obsession stalkers and victims are casual acquaintances (neighbors, co-workers) or even complete strangers (fan/celebrity). These stalkers seek to raise their own self-esteem by associating with those whom they hold in high regard. Love obsession stalkers become so focused on establishing a personal relationship with their victims that they often invent detailed fantasies of a nonexistent relationship. They literally script the relationship as if it were a Hollywood movie. However, when victims choose not to participate in the stalker's imagined passion film, the stalker may try to force victims into assigned roles. Often, love obsession stalkers are so desperate to establish

whether Nancy's admirer is a love obsession stalker and whether he also presents aspects of an erotomaniac stalker, as he may believe that he and Nancy are having a relationship (Casper Martinez, 2000). This episode can be complemented with several other clips from other TV shows and films dealing with stalkers. For example, in *There's Something About Mary* (Farrelly and Farrelly, 1998) Ted, who 13 years after graduation from high school still has a crush on—and probably even an obsession with—Mary hires a private investigator, Pat Healy to track her down. Healy follows Mary everywhere. He spies on her and eavesdrops on her conversations with her friends and family. He even makes contact with her.

Songs can also be used to analyze stories and events from a legal perspective. A popular culture song that deals with stalking is *Every Breath You Take* written by Sting and performed by The Police. The song tells the story of a stalker who is watching "every breath you take, every move you make, every bond you break, every step you take."

Another example to illustrate how to work with popular culture texts as sources for learning law and criminal justice is to use clips depicting trials from movies and TV shows. If, for example, you want students to learn about objections in trials, you can show some scenes for students to make objections while they watch the testimony of witnesses and the lawyers' examination and cross-examination of witnesses. You can divide the class in three groups. One group will be the defense lawyers, the other one will play the role of the prosecutor, and the third group will be the judge. You play the selected trial scenes and ask the first two groups of students to object at any time there are grounds for objections according to their roles. Apart from objecting, they have to state the grounds for the objection. The students playing the judge have to rule on the objection. For example, *My Cousin Vinny* (Lynn, 1992), like most courtroom movies, is plagued with objections and even more with grounds for objections not raised in court. This activity can also be used for the analysis of any aspect of the trial. As a way of illustration, you can show a trial up to the closing arguments, and ask students to prepare and present the closing arguments. Then you can show the closing arguments from the film or TV show and compare them to the ones presented by the students.

---

a relationship—*any relationship*—that they settle for negative relationships. Erotomaniacs delude themselves into believing that they already have a relationship with the objects of their obsession. Erotomania stalking cases often draw public attention because the target is usually a public figure or celebrity.

Another example to illustrate the way to teach with popular culture texts is to analyze constitutional and legal breaches in police investigation. For example, you can screen scenes from a film showing a police officer investigating a crime. Then, you can ask students to raise constitutional and legal challenges to police conduct. In this respect, you can show scenes from *Dirty Harry* (Siegel, 1971), where San Francisco Police Inspector "Dirty" Harry Callahan commits a series of police brutality acts in order to arrest a serial killer, including searching the suspect's home without a warrant, seizing his rifle, denying the suspect his right to seek legal counsel, and even torturing the suspect. Students can discuss whether a search warrant is needed and, if so, what legal consequences Dirty Harry's conduct triggers off. In an advanced class, students can watch *Charlie Chan's Chance* (Blystone, 1932). Charlie Chan investigates the murder of Sir Lionel Grey, a former head of Scotland Yard, who is killed in New York. The investigation involves gathering evidence in both the United States and England. Students can discuss bilateral, regional, and multilateral international agreements dealing with law enforcement and judicial assistance obligations in the investigation and prosecution of crimes with an international component. Students can do research about these agreements and can identify the benefits of these agreements for law enforcement. They can also identify the disadvantages of the existing framework that is applicable to Sir Lionel Grey's case. Students can propose the basis for law reform in the area so that police officers can have more rights and do a better job in investigating in this case and similar cases with international connections and effects.

In a criminal justice class, you can ask students to identify the theoretical criminal justice models that criminal justice agents, victims, and perpetrators from films and TV shows adhere to. Criminal justice models are theoretical frameworks to think about the criminal justice system. Most people, including many seasoned professionals, are unaware of their allegiance to one of these theoretical models, but their actions invariably align with one of the models. As a way of illustration, in *10 To Midnight* (Thompson, 1983) Detective Leo Kessler a seasoned police officer, plants evidence to help convict a serial killer. The defense lawyer presses his assistant, Detective Paul McAnn, who knows about Kessler's actions and agrees to testify against Kessler. This results in the exclusion of the false evidence from the trial. Students need to identify which criminal justice model each of the criminal justice agents adheres to. Students can also discuss Detective Kessler's actions and the legal consequences of planted evidence.

An interesting activity to teach the critiques to the eyewitness testimony and the unreliability of memory, problems of perception, and inaccuracy of crime perpetrators is to show a crime and ask students to pretend to give testimony about what they just saw. For example, you can show scenes from *Home Alone* (Columbus, 1990) where Harry and Marv burglarized vacant houses. Students have to identify what is missing from the houses, and any other information that they consider relevant for the investigation of the crime. Then, you can show the scenes again; and they can compare what they remembered with what actually happened, which will lead them to recognize the fragility of eyewitness testimony.

Another activity for a criminal justice class involves the analysis of crime scene investigations. You can show a film or TV show depicting a crime and the process followed by police officers in the scene of the crime. Then, you can ask students to analyze the way the investigation is conducted. Students can focus on whether the search for and collection of evidence are done according to procedure, whether the collection of evidence disturbs the crime scene and does not interfere with other evidence. Students can also focus on whether the police appropriately secure the crime scene, walks through the crime scene to get the big picture of the scene, and whether police officers formulate initial theories based on their visual examination of the crime scene. You can also ask students to examine whether the police officers neglect to collect some pieces of evidence and whether the documentation of the collected evidence is done appropriately.

5.8   SUMMARY

Academic disciplines tell stories: a general, foundational story that attracts and unites all members of the discipline and innumerable specific stories that apply and expand on the foundational story.

Law tells the story that it is possible to harmoniously regulate human behavior through laws and that professional third parties (judges) can enforce the law objectively and restore justice whenever someone breaches the law. Criminal justice tells the stories of police, the courts, and prisons.

Stories and storytelling permeate the practice of law and criminal justice. Clients, witnesses, police officers, prosecutors, lawyers, and judges tell stories. The paradigmatic story is the judicial case, where judges narrate the story of a dispute. Cases tell stories that deal with every single aspect of human life, including the most essential aspects of life. All cases narrate stories in dramatic ways and follow a structure that is not too dissimilar from the narrative structure of popular culture texts: setup (facts of the case), conflict (identification of legal issue, applicable rule, and legal analysis), and resolution (decision).

There is an abundance of popular culture stories such as films, TV shows, songs, and novels focused on law, lawyers, and the legal and criminal justice systems, which gave rise to the genre of popular legal culture. Its academic analysis, in turn, gave rise to the field of law and popular culture, which is concerned with the mutual influence that each exercises over the other. Despite the popularity of popular legal culture and the increasing importance of law and popular culture, popular culture texts are not used as sources for the study of law or criminal justice, which, in North America, is still based almost exclusively on the analysis of cases and criminal justice textbooks, respectively.

Teaching law and criminal justice with stories from popular culture constitutes a sound pedagogical alternative to reported cases and text-books, because they can greatly motivate students while at the same time they offer a wide array of diverse stories for students to examine substantive aspects of the legal and criminal justice disciplines.

The next chapter will examine the importance of teaching media literacy in the law and criminal justice classrooms. I will focus the discussion on the interpretation and production of popular culture and other media texts.

KEYWORDS

- **academic disciplines**
- **stories**
- **storytelling**
- **teaching with stories**
- **law and popular culture**
- **court cases**

CHAPTER 6

Popular Culture and Media Literacy in the Classroom

Public opinion doesn't have a law degree.

—House of Cards (2012)

ABSTRACT

Despite the importance which the production of popular culture and other media stories has for legal and criminal justice practice, higher education programs fail to help students develop media literacy and do not adequately prepare them to produce and analyze popular culture works and other media texts.

6.1 INTRODUCTION

As discussed in the previous chapter, the law and popular culture literature identified two gaps in the field: the use of popular culture works as primary sources for law teaching and the absence of the analysis of the conventions of legal popular culture in the law school and law-related university curricula (Elkins, 2007). The previous chapter dealt with the first issue. This chapter will focus on the second gap. Despite the importance that the production of popular culture and other media stories has for the legal and criminal justice practices, law schools and criminal justice university programs have traditionally neglected to prepare their students to be producers of popular culture and other media stories.

The objective of this chapter is to highlight the importance of helping students develop media literacy at the law school and criminal justice settings and to offer some examples of deep learning activities aimed at fostering media literacy in the law school and university contexts. I will start this chapter by discussing the role of lawyers and criminal justice agents in the production of popular culture stories and other media texts, including their participation in the construction of news stories and the production of media texts to use in connection with a case, such as video-taped depositions, videotaped crime scenes, a day-in-the life of videos, progressive videos, settlement brochures, living plaintiff documentaries, multimedia closing arguments, sentencing mitigation videos, visual petitions to administrative bodies, and clemency videos.

Because most of these audiovisual and media texts are used in court, I will also analyze the regulations to make these texts. I will then briefly examine the evolution of media literacy and its current marginal role in higher education. I will then stress the importance of teaching media literacy in legal and criminal justice education contexts. Finally, I will discuss some activities aimed at fostering the development of media literacy in law school and criminal justice university courses.

6.2   POPULAR CULTURE IN THE LEGAL AND CRIMINAL JUSTICE PROFESSIONS

In *Gone But Not Forgotten* (Mastroianni, 2005), Betsy Tannenbaum, a criminal defense attorney, knows how to play the press game. She knows the ethics rules and legislation in California that apply to lawyers in their relations with media. More important, she understands that media speak a language that is radically different from the language lawyers and criminal justice professionals speak. Betsy is always prepared to talk to the press. She knows she can expect reporters at any time—at her office, outside the courthouse, and at her clients' premises. She never avoids reporters. She is always ready. Every day at her office, Betsy Tannenbaum sits down and carefully prepares message points that she wants to communicate to the press. These are short and catchy statements, crafted in the language that reporters use. Each of these message points could be headlines in newspapers and magazine articles. When she talks to the press, she is highly articulate. She avoids legal jargon and long explanations about legal doctrine or procedure. If necessary, she is prepared to offer written brief explanations of her client's position. She is also aware of body language. She looks confident, yet friendly. She sounds assertive, polite, and intelligent. Most of the times, her statements are quoted in the press. Sometimes, they make headlines. When reporters insist on trying to make her say something that she does not agree with, she always comes back to her message points. For example, when questioned about her client's nonguilty verdict in a high profile battered woman syndrome defense case, Ms. Tannenbaum is concise, accurate, and quotable: "The verdict shows that a person has a right to defend herself." When pressed, when television, radio, and print media reporters insist and ask her if she believes that the verdict is unfair, if it means that murder is now legal, Betsy Tannenbaum stays on message. "[My client] was in a private battlefield of abuse. She had to make a stand to save her life."

Betsy is also a frequent guest in radio and television talk shows. She understands the special rhythm that radio and television impose. So, her answers are very concise—even more so than when she is interviewed by print media journalists. Still, her answers always leave the door open for further questions. Betsy is always dressed in impeccable outfits. She wears dark-colored skirted suits that fall at or below her knees. Her attires command respect, inspire trust, and convey a polished, professional image.

Her quotes in the media and her guest appearances in radio and television give her a unique marketing opportunity. Media coverage gives her recognition as an authority figure in criminal law. As part of her branding strategy, Betsy Tannenbaum has a proactive attitude toward media. She partners with a professional journalist, Nora Sloane (Robin Riker), to write the story of one of her clients and, indirectly, her own story. Betsy knows this will help her win her case, and at the same time, it will give her more media coverage and public recognition. Furthermore, she is aware that media exposure "plays a major role in reshaping public opinion, and ultimately, criminal justice policy" (Beale, 2006). For this purpose, Betsy spends hours talking to Norah about the case and about her life. She suggests Norah shadow her in court and in her office. In order to make the story more human and appealing to readers, Betsy agrees to let Nora interview Betsy's ex-husband (David Lee Smith). Betsy and Nora also agree to sit down and try to write part of the story together.

6.3 PRODUCERS OF POPULAR CULTURE AND MEDIA STORIES

Legal and criminal justice professionals are active producers of popular culture and other media stories. They contribute to news articles by answering questions to newspaper, magazine, and online reporters. They participate in television and radios news programs and talk shows. They offer their views in documentaries. They also write their own stories in press releases, websites, articles, and documentaries. Creating stories—both directly and indirectly—has become an essential aspect of their professional practice.

> Lawyers who represent clients in high-profile cases involving public figures must, where appropriate – and [...] always consistent with the canons of ethics and the rules of court - engage in their own press advocacy as part of their defense on behalf of a client (Bennet, 1996).

Lawyers produce stories directly and indirectly. They produce stories directly when they write press releases about their court victories or their participation in multimillion business deals, when they create a story for their websites, or when they tweet about their involvement in a case. They also create stories indirectly when they answer questions from reporters about their clients' cases or when they participate in radio talk shows or TV news programs commenting about legal developments or law reforms. Police officers and other criminal justice agents also deal with the press practically on an everyday basis.

6.4 LAWYERS AND CRIMINAL JUSTICE AGENTS AND THEIR DEALINGS WITH THE PRESS

Working with the press requires specific knowledge of the conventions that rule the media. The language that reporters speak is radically different from the language used in the courtrooms, law firms, and police headquarters. Journalists use words and phrases that lawyers and criminal justice professionals do not normally use. The layers of editing shape the stories in a way that is not common in legal and criminal justice circles. Journalists tend to get all sides of the story, whereas trial lawyers tend to advance their clients' positions (Cotter, 2010). What's more, each media outlet has its own idiosyncrasies, which lawyers and criminal justice agents need to know how to navigate.

There are also ethics rules governing lawyers' relations with media. For example, the American Bar Association Model Rule of Professional Conduct restricts lawyers' right to "make an extrajudicial statement that the lawyer knows or reasonably should know will be disseminated by means of public communication and will have a substantial likelihood of materially prejudicing an adjudicative proceeding in the matter."[1] The rules on maintaining the integrity of the profession also apply to lawyers' dealings with the media.[2] Most state bars and local associations also contain very detailed rules regulating lawyers' contact with the media. For example, in Ontario, Canada, the Law Society rules include a series of conditions that lawyers must satisfy before making public statements to the press.[3]

Working with the press requires careful preparation. Legal and criminal justice professionals need to prepare for their dealings with the press. This requires being informed about the big picture of the case and not just the angle of the lawyer's client or the specific investigation carried out by a police officer. If, for example, a police officer is investigating a new street drug in his jurisdiction, he must know if this drug is part of a new modality of drug consumption within a certain demographic. If a lawyer is defending a company accused of pollution in a certain industry, she should know about changes in the public perception of environmental risks in that industry. This preparation also requires crafting messages for media consumption that speak the language of the target media outlets. In general, these messages must be brief, precise, and accurate. They should be crafted in a language that is catchy and apt for being quoted in the press. In *Gone But Not Forgotten* (2005) Betsy Tannenbaum knows that media can help her get her message across to the largest audience possible. So,

---

[1] American Bar Association Model Rule of Professional Conduct, Section 3.6.
[2] American Bar Association Model Rule of Professional Conduct, Section 8.
[3] Public Appearances and Public Statements Communication with the Public 6.06 (1) Provided that there is no infringement of the lawyer's obligations to the client, the profession, the courts, or the administration of justice, a lawyer may communicate information to the media and may make public appearances and statements. Commentary: Lawyers in their public appearances and public statements should conduct themselves in the same manner as with their clients, their fellow legal practitioners, and tribunals. Dealings with the media are simply an extension of the lawyer's conduct in a professional capacity. The mere fact that a lawyer's appearance is outside of a courtroom, a tribunal, or the lawyer's office does not excuse conduct that would otherwise be considered improper. A lawyer's duty to the client demands that, before making a public statement concerning the client's affairs, the lawyer must first be satisfied that any communication is in the best interests of the client and within the scope of the retainer. Rules of Professional Conduct, Law Society of Upper Canada.

she always prepares clear, punchy, and catchy sentences that newspaper journalists love to quote in their articles and TV news anchors like to show in their news programs. Her statements are never boring. They have a hook that makes reporters keep asking her questions and that elicits invitations to radio call-in shows and TV talk shows.

In contrast, in *The Accused* (1988), assistant deputy prosecutor Kathryn Murphy treats the press as an obligation that she wants to get over with as soon as possible in order to get back to her investigation and prosecution. As a result, she is grilled by the press. Any minor mistake she makes is magnified by tabloids and TV news programs, which try to destroy her and her main witness in a major rape case.

6.5 INFLUENCE OF POPULAR CULTURE STORIES IN THE LEGAL AND CRIMINAL JUSTICE FIELDS

Apart from the importance of the press for the legal and criminal justice practices, popular culture stories and other media texts are pervasive in the legal and criminal justice professions in many other ways. At a general level, for example, media texts influence and even define the public notion of crime (Asimow and Mader, 2004). For example, the prevalence of crime drama shows on television has led the public to believe that crime is more rampant in society than it actually is (Mutz and Nir, 2009) and that the average person is more likely to become the victim of a crime, particularly of those offenses routinely portrayed in television such as street crimes and sex offences. Furthermore, popular culture crime films and series have contributed to the adoption of a law and order agenda and stricter legislation against these crimes (Dowler, Fleming, and Muzzatti, 2006). Popular culture stories also determine and disseminate a particular view of the criminal procedure and the role of lawyers and criminal justice agents. This view is so pervasive that there is a perceived expectation among the general public and criminal justice professionals that criminal proceedings must conform to the processes and actions routinely depicted in Hollywood films and television shows. Some legal and criminal justice professionals have shown concern about the fact that the gap between the image of the criminal justice system depicted in popular culture stories and the actual criminal justice system exerts pressure on their everyday professional practice to mirror popular culture stories, which has resulted in a more inefficient criminal justice system (Hughes and Magers, 2007; Owens, 2009). For example, with the advent of the *CSI* franchise, its spinoffs, and other similar shows that routinely depict the work of forensic laboratories that focus on DNA evidence used in criminal trial proceedings, jurors in the United States are not likely to render guilty verdicts in the absence of DNA or other forensic evidence (Owens, 2009). This phenomenon, referred to as the CSI effect, makes it more difficult to prove the guilt of an accused when DNA evidence is not available. Jurors, like the American television watchers, now expect the criminal trial to mirror popular culture's emphasis on DNA evidence (Owens, 2009).

Additionally, there are scores of research studies outside the United States that indicate that lay people and even some criminal justice professionals in countries which have a criminal procedure that differs from the American model believe that their criminal justice system is the same as in the United States.

TV and radio news programs also play a substantial role in determining the culpability of the accused and suspects.

> We live in an era where prosecutors use journalists to publicize their ongoing investigations, while journalists, through their news stories, can generate public and congressional demands for investigations and indictments from prosecutors. Many criminal prosecutions, particularly in political and business crime cases, are born in the pages of newspapers where investigative reporters, seeking to be the Woodwards and Bernsteins of their day, print titillating allegations, and where government agents who dislike the plea bargains struck by lawyers, leak information to the press in the hope that public attention will kill the deal (Bennet, 1996).

In high profile cases, it is difficult for a defense attorney or for the prosecutor to win a case in court without first obtaining a favorable media coverage in a phenomenon known as the court of public opinion. Media coverage of court cases and criminal investigations has the power to influence public opinion in favor of or against the accused. Legal and criminal justice professionals who understand the emotional rhetoric and passionate forces that catapult a case into media spotlight and who know how to navigate the complexities that control media can garner enough public support for their side in a court case or criminal investigation.

Documentaries also play a very important role in the law and criminal justice fields. Documentaries strongly influence people's perceptions about the law. They tend to form public opinion on most issues. For example, scores of documentaries on the perilous abuse of junk food such as *Super Size Me* (Spurlock, 2004), *Fast, Sick and Nearly Dead* (Cross and Engfehr, 2010), and *Hungry for Change* (Colquhoun, Ten Bosch and Ledesma, 2012) have contributed to create consciousness about unhealthy food habits, which led to many policy and legal changes such as the infamous Michael Bloomberg's ban against the sale of sodas larger than 16 oz. at restaurants, food carts, sports arenas, and movie theaters in New York city.

Similarly, many documentaries on the environment, such as *An Inconvenient Truth* (Guggenheim, 2006), *The Disenchanted Forest* (Siegel, 2002), and *Wild Horses* (Martin, 2013), among hundreds of others, have influenced public opinion and, in turn, have shaped public policy in a wide range of environmental areas—from the protection of wild animals to the safeguard of waters.

In some cases, documentaries directly affect the outcome of judicial decisions. For example, *Paradise Lost: The Child Murders at Robin Hood Hills* (Berlinger and Bruce Sinofsky, 1996) and its sequels narrate the trials of Jessie Misskelley, Damien Echols, and Jason Baldwin, known as the West Memphis Three, for their alleged murder and mutilation of three boys in West Memphis, Arkansas. The documentaries were instrumental in showing police and prosecutorial mistakes that contributed to the release of the West Memphis Three for time served.

> Paradise Lost acted as a catalysis for social change by creating the environment for a public concerned with miscarriages of justice while creating rhetorical identification with the convicted, "The West Memphis Three." In the film's absence, counter-narratives silenced in the official court hearings or by the corporate media would have never proliferated in a significant way. Hence, the documentary film acts as a means for counter-publics to create social change by transferring discourse from the private to the counter-public sphere (Aguayo, 2005).

6.6 PRODUCTION OF MEDIA TEXTS IN THE LEGAL AND CRIMINAL JUSTICE PROFESSIONS

At a more specific level, lawyers and other justice professionals must increasingly produce media texts in their everyday professional practice.

Because of the severe legal consequences of producing a video or another media text in the legal field, the lead lawyer in charge of the trial has full responsibility over the final product and thus assumes the role of director of the media text.

> "I–the lawyer– direct [a videotaped deposition.] … I don't care if the videographer thinks it will look better with the camera in one place or another. *I* decide where it goes, and I will live with the results. … It's the lawyer's rear end that's on the line. If my client wins, it's my doing. If my client loses, it's my doing. I'm the director, the producer … I the god of the deposition." (Paul Tauger, 2003).

> It is perfectly acceptable for a lawyer to outsource the production of the video. However, he (sic) must take care to never abdicate his (sic) role as director. Only the lawyer knows what will persuade the judge. Thus, he (sic) must always retain control of the story and its telling (Passon, 2010).

Media texts used in the legal and criminal justice professions include videotaped depositions, videotaped crime scenes, a day-in-the life videos, progressive videos, settlement brochures, living plaintiff documentaries, multimedia closing arguments, sentencing mitigation videos, visual petitions to administrative bodies, and clemency videos. Depositions are increasingly videotaped, particularly when the aim is to preserve testimony for trial.[4] Criminal justice professionals also routinely film, and take photographs of, crime scenes. They also film when investigating crimes in an undercover fashion. A day-in-the-life video is an audiovisual text aimed at accurately recording the injured party's activities of daily living. This video focuses on a daily routine, which is then edited to a 10- to 30-min tape. For instance, a tort lawsuit may involve a plaintiff who now must live her life being blind, deaf, or with a severe muscular injury, or constantly under mental anguish as a result of a beating and rape followed by fire to the plaintiff's house. The elements of pain and suffering, mental anguish, and loss of wages often are the most difficult aspects of a case for a jury to picture. Video is the most effective way to show pain and suffering or mental anguish. A day-in-the-life video can be shown in a torts lawsuit or as a part of a victim impact statement at sentencing hearings in criminal

---

[4]Experts consider that presenting videotaped deposition testimony at trial is the most effective alternative, and preferred over reading transcripts to the jury. Paul Tauger, "The Ultimate Video Deposition Skinny" (2003) available online at: http:// dvinfo.net/articles/business/tauger1.php.

justice processes. The progressive video is a modified type of day-in-the-life videos that show the pain and suffering of the plaintiff or victim over an extended period of time. Settlement brochures are more elaborate videos showing interviews of plaintiff's family and friends affected by the harm caused to the plaintiff. They present a chronological narration of the life of the plaintiff before and after the tort. They are used as a settlement strategy. Living plaintiff documentaries are also used to induce settlements. The documentary shows interviews with family members, employers, and friends along with edited photos and home videos, depicting plaintiff's life prior to the injury and the changes produced by the tort.

A multimedia closing argument is a closing argument made partially or entirely by means of photography, video, slides, drawings, and audio. It includes previously admitted evidence. And it aims to reconstruct the crime and the circumstances surrounding the crime. Its use has generated controversy and fascinating debates about its use in criminal trials.

Sentencing mitigation videos are audiovisual narratives of the defendant's life story used in sentencing hearings in order to persuade a judge of the existence of mitigating factors. At sentencing hearings, prosecutors describe the worst aspects of the defendant's life that led to the perpetration of the crime. A sentencing mitigation video contextualizes those aspects.

> The best stories, including the best sentencing stories, involve the protagonist battling against, and ultimately defeating, the antagonist forces (Passon, 2010).

Visual petitions to administrative bodies and clemency videos are audiovisual stories used in order to request an action from an administrative agency. A clemency video is a request made to the state governor for the lessening of the penalty of the crime without forgiving the crime itself, which is used mainly in capital punishment cases.

Other media texts increasingly used in the legal and criminal justice professions are documentaries related to a crime, a legal cause, or even a case under investigation or before the courts. The work of documentary filmmakers resembles the work of both academic researchers and creative screenwriters. Documentary filmmakers investigate facts, people, and events much like a researcher does, but they tell the product of their research through a story that uses film techniques rather than academic writing conventions. Documentaries, including documentaries with a legal focus, have distinctive technical film conventions and narrative structures.

Documentaries generally rely on a distinctive use of voiceover, archival footage of real events, reconstructions, natural sound and lighting, interviews with experts, montage, and texts on the screen to convey authority and credibility to the story. Apart from documentaries made by filmmakers to narrate stories based on their personal interests, clients have been increasingly asking lawyers to help them make documentaries as a means to get their stories across to media, the general public, and relevant governmental authorities.

6.7   REGULATIONS FOR THE USE OF MEDIA TEXTS IN THE LEGAL AND CRIMINAL JUSTICE FIELDS

Criminal justice system agencies, such as the courts, legislatures, and police have issued laws, rules, guidelines, and regulations that must be followed for media productions to be legally valid, particularly before the courts. These laws determine what types of camera movements, shots, angles, and editing are permitted. As a matter of illustration, California law contains extensive regulations dealing with the accepted ways of videotaping a deposition.[5] It clearly establishes the accepted procedures that must be followed, such as instructions to the video operator not to "distort the appearance or the demeanor of participants in the deposition by the use of camera or sound recording techniques."[6] For instance, the camera must show the witness's face and upper body (medium close up), the backgrounds must be simple, such as a neutral gray backdrop, or a simple textured backdrop. The lightings may not focus directly on the witness' eyes. The camera may not move (Tauger, 2003). California law also regulates the possibility of offering parts of a deposition as evidence in trials.

Similarly, the Royal Canadian Mounted Police (RCMP) has adopted regulations on crime scene photography. These regulations include a series of rules dealing with camera movement, lighting, and camera angles so that the photographs may be admitted in court[7].

---

[5]California Civil Code, Section 2025.
[6]California Civil Code, Section 2025.
[7]RCMP, Crime Scene Photography, available online at http://www.rcmp-learning.org/docs/ecdd1004.htm.

For the videotaping of crime scenes, the FBI counsels that the videographer "should describe on tape each room and view of the crime scene." According to the FBI, "common errors committed when videotaping a crime scene include panning the camera rapidly, poor focusing and lighting and improper use of the zoom feature of the cameras."

Courts have also contributed to the development and adoption of rules. For example, courts have invalidated day-in-the-life videos that show scenes filmed during more than a single day or which are too one-sided, giving the impression to jurors that the plaintiff is constantly in pain or that she is constantly suffering mental anguish.

Lawyers and criminal justice agents engaged in the production of media texts have described their approach to making audiovisual texts in the literature, which contributes to the creation of standard practices in the field (MacArthy, 2007).

> Sentencing videos should avoid using dramatic voice-over narrations, flashy editing tricks overbearing or melodramatic music, gratuitous scenes of crying loved ones, pointless inclusion of children, cheesy re-enactments, and so forth. This kind of overblown content distracts from the message of the film and wrecks credibility (Passon, 2010).

This combination of laws, guidelines, regulations, and standard practices has resulted in a film language that is unique to the legal arena.

6.8 MEDIA LITERACY AND THE MARGINS OF UNIVERSITY AND LAW SCHOOL EDUCATION

The rapid expansion of global communications media and visual culture in this digital era has shaken the structure of societies globally and has radically altered the dissemination and production of information and knowledge (Godlfarb, 2002). This revolution is fundamentally transforming our notions of education and learning. At the same time, it is altering the way we apprehend reality. It has changed the means people, particularly those who have grown up in this paradigm, use to communicate with one another, the concepts they form, and the structure of their thought (Lacy, 1982).

Media literacy places audiovisual languages at the forefront of classroom teaching and not as mere supplements to traditional classroom and print-based education (Godlfarb, 2002).[8] Media literacy recognizes the unique advantages that audiovisual media have as powerful transforming tools. When used as a tool in the classroom, the power of audiovisual media enables a level of interactivity and critical thinking not seen in traditional schooling (Goldfarb, 2002). Media literacy has been conceptualized as the "the process of critically analyzing and learning to create one's own messages – in print, audio, video, and multimedia, with emphasis on the learning and teaching of these skills through using mass media texts" (Hobbs, 1998). It includes the cognitive and affective processes involved in viewing and producing popular culture and other media texts. A media literate person is skillful in critically analyzing and creating popular culture stories and other media messages, examining media codes and conventions, identifying and criticizing stereotypes, values, and ideologies, and competent to interpret the multiple meanings and messages generated by popular culture and media texts (Keller, 2000).

Although there is a history of media education in Europe and North America that dates back to the end of the Second World War, media education has been at the margins of formal university teaching. Media literacy was developed in primary and secondary schools, as well as in vocational schools. In the last two decades, authors have been advocating for the development of media literacy across the university curriculum (Hobbs, 1998), and as part of a plan that is sensitive to the diverse concerns, knowledge, and experiences of students (Goldfarb, 2002). Just as education was transformed with the progress from oral to print literacy and book culture, the current technical revolution requires a radical transformation of education to give room to new literacies, curricula, and teaching goals (Keller, 2000). However, at the university setting, media literacy was relegated to some communications or film studies programs. It has not yet entered the curriculum in the majority of disciplines.

---

[8]Visual Pedagogy rejects the two predominant views—the Frankfurter school and Postmodernism—about the role of visual media in society. The Frankfurter School (Adorno, Horkheimer, Habermas References) considers popular culture and the mass media that produces it as one of the means of oppression by the power elites. The postmodernist view shifts responsibility from the makers and distributors of popular culture to the users who supposedly are able to critically read it and pick from it what they want and need for their social emancipation and subcultural identification. Visual Pedagogy shows that the use of media can have emancipatory effects in the short run as well as recuperative effects in the long run. Goldfarb (2002) posits that learning to critically read media texts is insufficient to take the ideological sting out of the message, but rejecting the use of media altogether is to deprive students of fundamental tools to apprehend the world surrounding them and to transform and affect it.

6.9   PRINT DOMINANCE IN LAW SCHOOLS

The patterns of modern Law School education were laid in an era of nearly total print dominance (Warner Lien, 1998). The educational concepts articulated were print-centered. Media literacy occupies a very limited and marginal role in North American law schools and with very few exceptions, such as the University of Pennsylvania Documentaries and the Law program, law schools do not teach their students the conventions of media language. "Writing and reading occupied a space of privilege in the Western tradition of education and literacy for the most of the twentieth century, making these skills key factors in subjects' identity and status relative to community" (Warner Lien, 1998).

In the last few decades, images have earned a new status in some educational contexts other than the law school and criminal justice programs. They have become a representational mode of choice well beyond their previous status as illustration. The visual has thus taken on a new importance not only in the scheme of knowledge representation but also in the formation of identity and community relative to how knowledge is accessed and lived (Weston and Cranton, 1986). Despite this slow change in paradigm, the prevailing teaching methods continue to be print-centered and focused on the teacher, whose role is still conceived as a major mediator between students and knowledge contained in published court decisions compiled in legal casebooks or in criminal justice textbooks (MacFarlane, 1994). The teaching methods do little, if anything, to encourage students to create and produce their own (and collective) media and popular culture legal or criminal justice texts (Le Brun and Johnstone, 1994).

6.10   INTERPRETATION OF POPULAR CULTURE STORIES AND OTHER MEDIA TEXTS IN THE CLASSROOM

The importance that popular culture stories and other media texts have in legal and criminal justice practice and the pervasiveness of popular culture texts make it necessary to help students acquire and develop media literacy skills in the law school and university classroom. These skills will help students interpret and produce media texts that are increasingly used in professional practice. At the same time, they help students become more proficient in reading popular culture texts, which, in turn, will help them with their analysis and discussion of law.

In order to achieve a high level of media literacy, you can help students both interpret and create media productions dealing with legal and criminal matters.

Interpreting popular culture texts is a complex and sophisticated process of actively working with the text. This process is shaped partly by the text, partly by the reader's background, and partly by the situation the interpretation occurs in (Hunt, 2004). Critical interpretation of a text requires students not to stop at the information explicitly contained in a text. "The explicit meanings of a piece are the tip of an iceberg of meaning; the larger part lies below the surface of the text and is composed of the reader's own relevant knowledge" (Hirsch, 1987).

A critical interpretation process is only possible if the interpreter uses a series of categories of analysis, some of which are common to most professional and academic communities (general categories of analysis) and some of which are specific to each academic discipline or professional field. The expert interpreter has incorporated these categories and applies them almost intuitively. But most students—particularly lower year students—ignore them. So, we need to teach both the general analytical tools and the discipline-specific values and strategies that facilitate the critical interpretation of popular culture stories with legal and criminal justice themes. The critical interpretation process also requires expressly teaching students the conventions of film language, including camera movements, angles, editing techniques, and sound effects, the meanings they can convey, media narrative structure, and media discourse. This also calls for helping students develop the skills that are necessary to realize how media construct legal meanings, influence, and educate both legal and lay audiences, and impose their messages and values in every dimension of the legal and criminal justice worlds.

6.11 GENERAL CATEGORIES FOR THE INTERPRETATION OF POPULAR CULTURE STORIES

General categories of analysis are tools that help students think, discuss, and interact with popular culture texts (Table 6.2).

General categories of analysis to interpret popular culture texts include the following: (1) purpose; (2) connections to other texts, including the context; (3) deconstruction of assumptions; (4) message; and (5) stereotypes.

6.11.1 PURPOSE

A critical analysis of a popular culture is pursued with a specific purpose, for example, to explore the image of prosecutors in courtroom dramas, to examine the image of judges as cultural symbols, or to analyze the notion of crime in popular culture. As novice critical interpreters of popular culture, when students—particularly lower year students—read a popular culture text, they do not have a purpose of their own. They approach the text because their teachers tell them to do so. So, as discussed in Chapter 2, we need to create problems, questions, or situations that students will feel motivated to solve or answer, and for which finding the solution or answer will create the need to interpret popular culture texts. In this case, students will approach a text in order to do something other than view the text to comply with external requirements or to have fun.

6.11.2 CONNECTIONS TO OTHER TEXTS

Popular culture texts are never produced in isolation. They have implicit and explicit connections to other texts. The content creator[9] refers to other films, TV shows, theater plays, songs, articles, or books. Thus, the meaning of a text does not depend solely on the content of the text itself. It depends in large part on its relations with these other—prior, contemporary, and subsequent—discourses (del Rosal, 2009). But students, particularly those in the lower years, ignore most of these connections. So, they need to become aware of the importance of identifying these connections. One of the most important connections is the context. Understanding the context helps students understand the background, environment, and circumstances in which the popular culture story was produced. In order

---

[9]I will use the term content creator to refer to all creators of popular culture stories, including directors, writers, composers, and authors. Similarly, I will use the term viewer to refer to the reader, listener, and audience of a popular culture story.

to analyze the context of any given text, students need to be encouraged to do some research about the authors, producers, directors, and actors. Students need to analyze the audience of the text as well as when and where the text was created.

Table 6.1 defines the possible connections of a popular culture text with other texts. Although some of these connections may not be present in all popular culture stories, awareness of these possible connections which a text may have facilitates critical interpretation of popular culture texts.

TABLE 6.1 Connections of a Text.

Text	The information explicitly provided by the content creator.
Context	The historical, cultural, political, and social background of the text.
Subtext	The content creator's purpose, agenda, and voice.
Intertext	The connections between the text and other texts.
	• Horizontal intertext: the connections between the viewer and the content creator.
	• Vertical intertext: the connections between the text and other texts (prior, contemporary, and subsequent).
Hypertext	The links to other texts or to other parts of the text.
Pretext	The ideological assumptions which the viewer brings to the text.
The repressed text	The texts that the content creator consciously or unconsciously fails to consider and incorporate in his or her text.

6.11.3 DECONSTRUCTION OF ASSUMPTIONS

Popular culture texts assume certain concepts, ideas, and principles. They rely on the knowledge that is already common among many viewers of popular culture stories. Students need to be aware that they need to uncover these assumptions. If they do not know some of these taken-for-granted ideas and concepts, they need to investigate them.

Another important factor in helping students become immersed in the critical interpretation of popular culture stories is knowledge background. Hirsch refers to this knowledge background as cultural literacy, which he defines as "the network of information that all competent readers possess. It is the background information, stored in their minds, that enables them to pick up a newspaper and read it with an adequate level of comprehension, getting the point, grasping the implications, relating what they read to the unstated context, which alone gives meaning to what they read" (Hirsch, 1987). We need to know where students are and help them both activate and increase their knowledge background. The richer their knowledge background is, the deeper their understanding of a popular culture story is.

6.11.4 MESSAGE

Students also need to learn how to identify the message or messages of the popular culture story. Students need to learn how to identify the main message and the elements the content creator uses to advance this message. One of the most important aspects of critical interpretation of popular culture stories is evaluating the message. Many students tend to view popular culture stories without ever questioning them. Thus, students need to learn to challenge the messages popular culture stories convey. Another factor that helps students evaluate the message consists of identifying the hidden or repressed texts or ideas. In most popular culture stories, the author consciously or unconsciously ignores or fails to consider other ideas, angles, and arguments that directly or indirectly deal with the text's message. Uncovering these repressed ideas helps students better assess the message by considering the full spectrum of ideas, concepts, and arguments that surround the message the content creator of the popular culture story is trying to make.

It is also important to recognize the effects that the message directly or indirectly produces on the viewer and to analyze whether the content creator intends to produce those effects in the audience.

6.11.5 STEREOTYPES

Stereotyping is an oversimplified view of a group. Stereotyping is a narrative convention frequently used in popular culture. It helps the content creator with the rhythm of the story, as he or she does not have to explain all the features of a character. The content creator simply gives the character the characteristics of the group. In most cases, stereotyping embraces racist beliefs (Quintana, 2015). For example, if the perpetrator of a robbery is a poor Mexican illegal alien, the popular culture story is using a stereotype that many Mexican illegal aliens are criminals. This, of course, does not reflect the fact that the overwhelming majority of Mexican illegal aliens are not criminal offenders.

The negative effects of stereotypes are not only "the repetition of distorted imagery, but also the omission of diverse imagery" (Alsultany, 2013). If popular culture stories depict only white mainstream males as successful, rich, and educated, they transmit the message that people from other backgrounds are not successful. Students need to recognize stereotyping in popular culture stories. At the same time, they need to be aware of the power relations that the stereotyping conveys in the story.

TABLE 6.2 General Categories of Analysis for the Interpretation of Popular Culture Texts.

1. What is the purpose for reading/viewing this text? Is it entertaining? Is it to explore an approach, theory, or concept? Is it to understand an aspect described or referred to in the text?

2. What are the connections to other texts? What is the relation of the text with other—prior, contemporary, and subsequent—texts?

3. What is the context of the text? What are the background, environment, and circumstances in which the content creator produced the text?

4. What assumptions does the text make? What does it take for granted? What do I need to know to uncover these assumptions?

5. What is the message of the text? What does the content creator want to tell the audience? What are the flaws of this message? What are the consequences of this message? What media language conventions, such as camera movements, backgrounds, lighting, editing, music, among others, does the content creator use to convey the message? What effect does the message have on me? Does the content creator intend to produce those effects in the audience?

6. What stereotypes does the text make? What generalizations does it make? Is the stereotype accurate? Is diverse imagery omitted? Who has been omitted? What group has been repressed? What relations of power does the text transpire?

6.12 LAW AND CRIMINAL JUSTICE SPECIFIC CATEGORIES OF ANALYSIS

In order to analyze popular culture stories related to law and criminal justice, it is also necessary to employ some categories of analysis that reflect the way in which legal and criminal justice practitioners think, express thoughts, and act in their professional lives (Table 6.3). A specific category of analysis is a framework to evaluate those thoughts and the discourse from within the legal and criminal justice fields. As with general categories of analysis, a legal or criminal justice expert has incorporated these categories. He or she analyzes a popular culture work by unconsciously sifting through it with a colander of categories of analysis.

The following categories of analysis, formulated as questions, can help students interpret a popular culture text critically.

TABLE 6.3   Specific Categories of Analysis.

(1) Are the legal references, such as the notion of crime, the criminal procedure, and legal doctrine, made in the popular culture story accurate from a legal point of view? Are there any generalizations or oversimplifications? How do the depictions of lawyers and other criminal justice agents differ from reality?
(2) Are there any relevant legal aspects that have been omitted in the popular culture story?
(3) What are the ethical considerations and implications related to the work of legal and criminal justice agents in the popular culture story? Do they show an understanding of ethical rules? Do they ignore them? Do they abide by them?
(4) What is the criminal justice model that predominates in the popular culture story? Does it prejudice the outcome of the crime?
(5) Is the popular culture story biased?

6.13   CLASS ACTIVITIES AIMED TO HELP STUDENTS INTERPRET POPULAR CULTURE AND OTHER MEDIA TEXTS

There are many class activities that you may propose students to do for the analysis of popular culture stories dealing with legal and criminal justice themes and issues. For this purpose, when carrying out any of the activities discussed in the previous chapter, you can extend the substantive discussions of legal issues to consider the technical aspects that contribute to narrate the story. For example, when analyzing the crime of stalking through the *Family*'s episode *Someone's Watching* (1977) mentioned in Chapter 5, you can ask students to complement this analysis by focusing on the conventions of film language and popular culture narrative to deconstruct how the director tells the story of a male law school student who stalks an attractive female colleague. Students can examine the film conventions (camera movements, angles, editing, and music) to convey the film's message. They can also analyze the context of the TV show, the lack of legislation about stalking, police attitude, and the public perception of this behavior when the show was made (1977). Students can examine the assumptions taken for granted in the TV show, the connections to future real cases, to other films on stalking, to news programs reporting about these cases, and to the vast body of criminological theory dealing with stalkers. Students can also analyze the stereotypes present in the episode: the male offender and the attractive female victim. More important, students can explore what the TV show leaves out in its story, what has been repressed, and what is not told.

Another activity can deal with the analysis of a day-in-the life video. For example, you can make a day-in-the-life of video by selecting relevant scenes from the movie *Speak* (Sharzer, 2004) that tells the story of a high-school student, Melinda Sordino, who is sexually assaulted during a party. This video may have both legal problems and editing mistakes for students to identify. As a matter of illustration, the scenes can take place in several days. In addition, they can only show situations where Melinda is depressed. Students would have to identify that the video should contain scenes filmed over a single day and that it should paint a complete picture of Melinda's life. It should also show her when she is not very depressed, which takes place when she connects to her Arts teacher. The technical analysis of media conventions must embrace the scrutiny of the rules and guidelines dealing with the camera movements, backgrounds, lighting, and editing for days in the life videos to be admitted in a court proceeding. You can also show students other videotaped depositions for them to analyze.

You can use real depositions, you can produce your own, or you can take them from feature films and TV shows, such as *The Deposition* (Mensore, 2011), *The Social Network* (Fincher, 2010), and *The Office*'s episode *The Deposition* (Farino, Season 4 Episode 8, 2007), among many others. These depositions can also have problems for students to identify. For example, you can produce a deposition where the camera moves from the deponent to the lawyer, then to the library that is behind the deponent, and then back to the deponent. In another deposition, you can show several close-ups of the deponent, particularly when the lawyer believes that the deponent is lying. Students should be able to realize that these camera movements and the close-ups do not follow the film language conventions of depositions, and, for this reason, they may be legally challenged.

6.14 PRODUCTION OF MEDIA TEXTS IN THE CRIMINAL JUSTICE AND LAW SCHOOL CLASSROOMS

There are several activities that you can do in class to help students produce popular culture and other media texts with a legal or criminal justice focus. Continuing with the examples described above, after students analyze the day-in-the-life video made from *Speak*, you can ask students to produce a video without legal and editing mistakes. Similarly, students can produce a deposition that respects the technical and legal requirements.

Another activity can deal with the production of documentaries with a legal or criminal justice focus. For example, you can ask students to do research on criminal events that may have taken place in the neighborhood surrounding the school campus. Students can then make a documentary and use the conventions of documentary films, such as the re-enactment of the criminal events, interviews with police officers, prosecutors, defense attorneys and judges, and footage obtained from TV news programs. Another example is to ask students to choose a legal cause such as the wrongful conviction of specific person, the over-incarceration of a certain minority group, a corruption case of a government official, the existence of a series of hate crimes against a certain group, the need for law reform in a certain area, or the need to adopt measures to better protect the rights of victims in the criminal trial process. Students can then make a documentary advocating for this cause. Another alternative is to focus on the historical analysis of a legal issue. For example, students can produce a documentary about the development of sexual assault legislation, victim-centered reforms, or antiterrorism measures.

All these activities help students acquire the skills necessary to interpret and produce their own media texts in the legal and criminal justice contexts. Teaching the conventions of film language and the actual analysis of these conventions, alongside the analysis of substantive disciplinary contents, gives students the necessary tools to become fully fledged legal and criminal justice professionals.

6.15   SUMMARY

The revolution in media and global communications in the last few decades has transformed the very basic foundations of knowledge and education. Global citizens of today and tomorrow need to be equipped with the necessary skills to both interpret and produce media texts, including popular culture works. North American universities as well as their European counterparts, with a teaching philosophy built during an exclusively print-centered era, have not yet fully opened their classroom doors to media literacy. The patterns of modern law school education were also laid in an era of nearly total print dominance. The educational concepts articulated were print-centered, where the main objective of law schools has been to dissect published edited appellate court decisions, and then to use this skill to achieve mastery of legal thought over a body of learning that itself had been shaped and disciplined by its reduction to print.

Media literacy occupies a very limited and marginal role in North American law schools and criminal justice programs, and with the exception of a few schools, practically no law school or criminal justice university program teaches its students the conventions of media language.

Lawyers as well as criminal justice professionals are currently involved in the production and analysis of media texts. These texts have a specific language, which substantially differs from the language used in other media contexts, such as feature films, documentaries, or anthropological interviews. Furthermore, most of these media products must show a strict adherence to the rules governing the language of media texts so that they may be used in court. In order to foster the development of well-prepared future legal and criminal justice professionals, we need to teach our students the conventions of media language so that they can be effective interpreters and producers of media texts.

In the next chapter, I will examine the concept of metacognition and its role in the deep learning process. I will analyze the general metacognition tools and specific metacognition resources to reflect on law and criminal justice. I will also discuss how to interpret and process popular culture stories to enhance deep learning.

KEYWORDS

- media literacy
- media stories
- print dominance
- dealing with the press
- categories of analysis
- interpretation of media texts
- production of media texts
- interpretation of media texts

CHAPTER 7

Metacognition

The past is just a story we tell ourselves.

—Her (Jonze, 2014)

ABSTRACT

Metacognition is the process of reflecting about and monitoring one's own learning. Mastering metacognitive reflection permits learners to become autonomous professionals and to be able make changes while learning. Metacognition, which is also part of the deep learning process, allows learners to recognize their own limitations of knowledge and to reflect about what they need to do in order to improve their professional practice. Learning how our brains interpret and process stories helps students develop metacognitive skills. It is also important for students to learn about the unconscious mechanisms that affect the understanding of stories, which includes priming, stereotyping, the mere exposure effect, and mental methods to deal with anomalies, contradictions, and gaps in the input story.

7.1 INTRODUCTION

The deep learning process requires constant feedback. Formative feedback has a marginal role in North American law schools and occupies a somewhat marginal place in criminal justice university programs. Still, some law school and university teachers give students feedback in their courses. This feedback tells them what they are doing well and where they need to improve. In some cases, teachers also tell students what they need to do to improve. Teacher feedback and information are essential for student learning. But once students graduate, they do not have their teachers by their side to give them feedback. Thus, students need to learn how to reflect about their own learning endeavors and to obtain information about their progress in the learning process.

I will begin this chapter with a brief conceptualization of metacognition, which is the most useful tool to reflect about one's learning process, and its connection to deep learning. Then, I will examine its main elements: awareness, knowledge, control, and emotion. I will also analyze the tools to carry out metacognitive reflection and some examples of metacognitive resources to learn law and criminal justice. Because stories, including popular culture stories, play an essential role in teaching and learning law and criminal justice, I will also examine how we interpret and process stories in our brains. Knowledge of these processes helps students in their metacognitive reflection.

7.2   METACOGNITION AND DEEP LEARNING

Metacognition consists of reflecting about and monitoring one's own learning process. Metacognition also includes recognizing our limitations of knowledge and what we need to do in order to keep learning to progress in the professional legal and criminal justice fields. Metacognitive reflection permits learners to make changes along the way. In practice, metacognition can be achieved through a series of tools, questions, elements, and other resources that facilitate the reflection on one's learning processes. This reflective practice leads to self-evaluation, which enables a process of lifelong learning.

7.3   METACOGNITION ELEMENTS

In *Makers: Lisa Leslie* (2014), we get a glimpse of Lisa Leslie's basketball career. Lisa was a passionate and remarkable player who reflected constantly about the game and analyzed every move inside and outside the court. Lisa also carefully analyzed all aspects of her career. She knew what she wanted to do. She even wrote down her career goals—and stuck to them—at a time when professional basketball for female players was not a possibility in the United States. Lisa always had a concrete plan to achieve her goals. When she got cut from the US Olympic team in 1990, she was disappointed. But instead of letting her disappointment stall her career, she went back to the drawing board, worked harder in the gym, and played as many games as she could to improve her skills. Two years later, she was cut from the Olympic team again. She kept improving her skills until finally she made the team and won the gold medal in four consecutive Olympic Games: Atlanta 1996, Sydney 2000, Athens 2004, and Beijing 2008.

She reflected alone. And she also talked about basketball with her coaches and team members. She engaged in meaningful conversations with the coach and team players, which helped her improve the depth of her incessant reflections about the game. When Lisa was on the court, she knew how to find a few seconds to think of the best play to help her team. Furthermore, Lisa knew how to learn from her mistakes. She reflected about them on and off the court. Sometimes, she even made changes to her game while she was playing. And she also helped her team members correct their plays.

There are four key components of metacognition: awareness, knowledge, control, and emotion. Awareness refers to the process of learning about one's cognitive structure. Lisa Leslie was aware of her basketball skills. She knew very well what she was capable of doing on the court. She knew what she needed to do to improve with practice. And she was also aware of her limitations. When Lisa realized that she was not young enough to go on playing professional basketball, she went back to school to pursue a master's degree in business to reinvent herself as a team co-owner. Metacognitive awareness also entails learning how to set one's own learning goals. In law school and university, teachers generally set those goals. Teachers tell students what aspects of the discipline they need to learn. For example, law schools have designed a curriculum that contains all of the skills, competences, concepts, principles, cases, and methods that students will need to master in order to graduate and become lawyers. But in order to be prepared for life outside law school, students themselves need to learn how to set their own learning goals.

Knowledge implies knowing about the learning process and knowing about one's own personal learning styles. Students need to learn about the process of knowledge construction and deep learning, which were discussed in previous chapters. They need to know that the deep learning process is produced when a learner faces a problem, question, or situation embedded in a story that creates a cognitive conflict when the learner interacts with peers. Students must be aware that they need to make higher order cognitive connections between the input story and their existing stories and that they need to reflect about the changes that occur as a result of this process. Students also need to know how human beings process and interpret stories and how some psychological and stereotyping phenomena affect the understanding of stories, which I will discuss in depth later in this chapter.

Control means monitoring one's own learning progress. It helps students correct themselves and make changes while they are engaged in their learning process. This aspect of metacognition is key to successful professional practice. It takes place when a lawyer or criminal justice professional reflects in action and as a consequence changes his or her tasks to correct something that he or she perceives that is not going well. This reflection and changes occur while the legal or criminal justice professional is actually conducting these tasks. For example, if a police officer is interrogating a suspect and she senses that the interrogation is going nowhere, she can change her interrogation strategy to elicit valuable information from the suspect.

The emotional element of metacognition requires students to pay attention to the feelings and emotions that learning something new generates and to recognize how these feelings affect them. Understanding all these feelings and emotions and how they affect what you do is essential for the deep learning process.

7.4   METACOGNITION TOOLS

Metacognitive reflection about the learning process must satisfy some conditions in order to be effective. First, learners must recognize their initial conceptions about law and criminal justice. Because most of these conceptions are implicit, the learner must reflect about them and get to explain them. Second, the learner must evaluate his or her conceptions and beliefs in light of the new conceptions that are being learned. Third, the learner must decide—consciously or unconsciously—whether or not he or she will restructure his or her initial conceptions (Carretero, 2009). For this purpose, students need information about their learning processes. We need to create opportunities for students to receive information from multiple sources, including peers, lawyers, criminal justice professionals, and other experts. For example, students could engage in tasks that legal and criminal justice professionals usually do. These professionals could observe the students and provide them with constructive feedback. Students should also learn to make pauses in their activities and reflect about them.

Like other phases of the deep learning process, metacognition entails both individual and social instances. The learner must find moments to reflect alone but must also seek opportunities to reflect about the learning process with peers.

7.5 GENERAL METACOGNITIVE QUESTIONS

Metacognitive tools are both general and discipline specific. General metacognition categories deal with how learners construct knowledge. A good way to present metacognitive tools to students is through questions that they can ask themselves throughout the learning process. These questions apply to virtually any academic discipline and not just to law or criminal justice. The following questions can be used with respect to any problem, question, or situation embedded in the input story that students deal with in any discipline.

TABLE 7.1 General Metacognitive Categories of Analysis.

(1)	What do I know about this problem, question, or situation? What is my first reaction or gut feeling? How can I instinctively solve the problem, answer the question, or analyze the situation now?
(2)	What new information or knowledge do I need in order to solve the problem, answer the question, or analyze the situation effectively?
(3)	What conversations and discussions do I need to have with my peers about the problem, question, or situation?
(4)	What analysis do I need to do with the new information or knowledge?
(5)	How can I relate what I already know and the new information or knowledge? What connections can I make?
(6)	How can I solve the problem, answer the question, or analyze the situation now?
(7)	How do my gender, race, ethnicity, and other social factors influence my solution to the problem, answer to the question, or analysis of the situation?
(8)	How does my new solution, answer, or analysis differ from my original, gut-feeling, response?

TABLE 7.1 *(Continued)*

(9)   Am I aware of mental mechanisms, such as priming, stereotyping, the mere exposure effect, and mental methods that deal with anomalies, contradictions, and gaps in the input story that may be affecting my understanding of the input story or the solution to the problem, answer to the question, or analysis of the situation?

(10)   What do I know now that I did not know before about the problem, question, or situation? What can I do now that I could not do before?

(11)   What do I know now about the discipline that I did not know before? What connections can I now make to the general framework of the discipline? What connections can I now make to other disciplines?

(12)   How can I use what I now know to solve other problems, answer other questions, or analyze other situations in the discipline? How can I transfer what I now know outside the discipline? How can what I now know help me solve everyday problems, answer everyday questions, and analyze everyday situations?

(13)   Where does this new knowledge place me within the discipline? What conversations can I now have with my peers and the discipline?

(14)   How has knowing what I now know impacted me? How does my solution, answer, or analysis affect me and others? How have I felt throughout this process? What emotions have I experienced? Does knowing what I know now change my attitude toward other people I know outside the discipline or outside academia?

(15)   What new questions do I have now about the original problem, question, or situation? What new questions do I have now about the discipline? What new personal goals do I now have about the discipline?

7.6   DISCIPLINE-SPECIFIC METACOGNITIVE QUESTIONS

Discipline-specific metacognitive categories have to do with the way law or criminal justice organizes and constructs knowledge, what questions the discipline asks, what method it uses to generate knowledge, what kind of conversation its members engage in, and what limitations the discipline has. It also deals with knowledge about the hidden structure of the discipline, that is to say, the layered characteristics of the discipline that lie beyond the surface (Perkins, 2009).

A good way to help students reflect about discipline-specific metacognitive categories is through questions. Table 7.2 shows some examples of metacognitive questions to assist in the reflection on the analysis of judicial court opinions. Table 7.3 contains some questions for the metacognitive reflection of problems and situations from diverse legal perspectives and legal traditions. Table 7.4 includes metacognitive questions designed to help students reflect about their learning process in criminal justice courses.

You can create similar questions for the reflection about the learning of other legal and criminal justice skills, concepts, and methods. All these questions give a general idea of how to formulate other metacognitive questions. They can be adapted to specific circumstances and learning goals. Not all questions will be relevant for every single issue that students are learning. You should discard those questions that are irrelevant and add new ones that suit what you want your students to deal with. For some students, these questions may be too detailed. For others, they may be too vague. Ideally, students should gradually learn to create new questions that will help them think about their own thinking and learning so that they can use the standards of the legal and criminal justice disciplines to recognize shortcomings and correct their reasoning as they go.

TABLE 7.2 Metacognitive Questions for Rule-Based Analysis of Judicial Cases.

(1)	Does the rule-based analysis originate from a case or a statute? How does this affect the analysis?
(2)	What is the rule? Which conception of rule am I dealing with?
(3)	What are the elements of the rule? Are all the elements present in the case?
(4)	What is the result?
(5)	What is the causal connection (mandatory, prohibitory, and discretionary) between the elements and the result?
(6)	Does the rule have any exceptions that would defeat the result even if all the elements are present?
(7)	In which way does the legal rule treat the elements (all required elements, alternative elements, or factor test)? If there is a factor test, what are the competing interests that have to be balanced and weighed to reach the conclusion determined by the rule?
(8)	Can I prove each element of the rule to be true or false?
(9)	Does the rule apply to the given set of facts?
(10)	Can I break down the elements of the rule into separate elements? Can I match the facts and circumstances of the case with each element of the rule to see if the element is proven?
	(a) Does this fact prove or disprove an element of the rule?
	(b) Does this particular circumstance prove or disprove the element of the rule?
	(c) Do the facts suggest a counterargument?

TABLE 7.3 Metacognitive Questions for the Analysis of Problems and Situations from Diverse Legal Perspectives and Legal Traditions.

(1)	Am I approaching the problem, question, or situation under several notions of law or only under legal positivism?
(2)	Am I exploring comparative law solutions? Am I taking into account international aspects of the problem, question, or situation?
(3)	Am I making connections to other legal phenomena, or am I only analyzing the problem, question, or situation in isolation?
(4)	Am I applying or taking into consideration the relevant legal theory/ies, or am I simply analyzing the problem, question, or situation from my common sense?
(5)	Am I taking into consideration the contributions of other social sciences to the problem, question, or situation? Or am I analyzing it exclusively from a legal perspective?
(6)	Am I considering the implications and applications of the problem, question, or situation, including policy considerations, or am I simply coming to conclusions without taking into account the implications and applications of the problem, question, or situation?
(7)	Am I critically analyzing the reasoning method surrounding the problem, question, or situation, or am I just taking for granted the validity of the reasoning method?

TABLE 7.4 Metacognitive Questions for Criminal Justice.

(1)	What is the criminal justice model that underlines my understanding of the problem, question, or situation? Is the problem, question, or situation explained under a certain criminal justice model? Would I see it differently if I approached the problem, question, or situation from a different criminal justice model?
(2)	What is the notion of crime that underlines my understanding of the problem, question, or situation? Is the problem, question, or situation explained under a certain notion of crime, perhaps the mainstream, legalistic, notion of crime? Would I see it differently if I approached the problem, question, or situation from a different notion of crime?
(3)	What criminology theory underlines my understanding of the problem, question, or situation? Is the problem, question, or situation explained under a certain criminological view/theory? Would I see it differently if I approached the problem, question, or situation from a different criminological view or theory?
(4)	If statistics are involved, am I aware of the possible flaws in the collection of criminal data? Would my understanding of the problem, question, or situation change if the statistics were not correct?

TABLE 7.4 *(Continued)*

(5)   Is the problem, question, or situation affected by criminal justice bias? For example, if minority groups are being arrested more in a certain area, does this mean that they are committing more crimes, or are the police arresting minority groups more than mainstream individuals?

(6)   Am I making connections to other criminal problems, questions, or situations, or am I only analyzing the problem, question, or situation in isolation?

(7)   Am I applying or taking into consideration criminological theories or criminal justice theoretical models, or am I simply analyzing the problem, question, or situation from my common sense?

(8)   Am I considering the implications and applications of the problem, question, or situation, or am I simply coming to conclusions without taking into account the implications and applications of the problem, question, or situation?

(9)   Am I critically analyzing the reasoning method surrounding the problem, or am I just taking for granted the validity of the reasoning method?

(10)   Am I exploring solutions to the problem in other countries? Am I taking into account any international aspects of the problem?

7.7 HOW WE PROCESS STORIES

As discussed throughout the book, stories, including popular culture stories, play an essential role in human learning and should also play an important role in teaching and learning law and criminal justice. Thus, learning about how we process stories is an essential aspect of the meta-cognitive reflection.

Cognitive psychology has long examined this process. Legal scholarship also paid attention to how human beings process stories in the context of jury deliberations and decisions. Probably, this is so because legal academics believe that judges, lawyers, and other legal and criminal justice professionals can be more objective and can interpret legal stories in a different, more professional way. Research shows that all human beings process stories in the same way, as we all have the same brain. Surely, our own worldview, including our professional education, constitutes a unique knowledge structure (which also includes our experiences and everything that we learned represented in our brains by innumerable neuronal synapses). But the neurological mechanism through which we connect that knowledge structure with a story we watch, read, or listen to is exactly the same in all individuals.

As discussed before, we process new information such as evidence in a criminal trial, what a client tells us about his marriage breakdown, or the instructions from a criminal justice superior, by placing that new information into story format (Blume et al., 2007). Then, that story activates an index of labels through which we have processed prior stories (our experiences and everything that we learned). After that, our brain selects an existing story to connect with the input story (Schank, 2000). So, for example, in *Law and Order Criminal Intent*'s episode *Senseless* (2007 S7 E 10) Felix has a history of rejections and failures. A high school drop out, Felix has had a few minimum-wage jobs, which he cannot keep for more than a few weeks. He has formed a gang to mask his failures. He has been arrested several times for theft and other offenses, as a result of which he faces a deportation order. His single mother does not care much about him. She thinks he is a loser and has neglected him. Felix is full of anger. He hates those who think that they are better than him. This is his existing story. This is what is in his cognitive structure. When Felix and two other members of his gang see Naomi Johnson (Monique Lea) and his brother in a park, Felix steals Naomi's iPhone. She is angry and calls Felix a "loser." This prompts Felix's story about his failures and rejections. When Naomi mentions the word "loser" Felix's brain rapidly scans his index of labels under which he has stored all his stories. There is a match between Naomi's story and the story of his mother's rejection and neglect. Both stories are indexed in Felix's brain under the same label (loser). So, Felix responds to Naomi's story by shooting her. Fortunately, not all of us react by shooting others. But we all link an input story with an existing story if there is a match between them. Thus, understanding depends on our previous stories. If someone calls me a loser, I will instantly laugh and think of the day when I missed a penalty kick in soccer finals when I was in high school. This is probably the only story that I stored under the label "loser" in my brain. "Different people understand the same story differently precisely because the stories they already know are different" (Schank, 2000). In other words, our existing stories influence our connections to, and understanding of, the new story. In some extreme cases, if the new input story has no points of connection with any of our existing stories, then we cannot process that story. We will simply ignore it and dismiss it. This is what happens, for example, when someone speaks to us in a language that we do not speak. If motivated enough, we may find some connections, such as cognates, body language, and other linguistic or paralinguistic clues. But if we are not motivated, we will not be able to make any connections. In many aspects, a new academic or professional discipline such as law and criminal justice may act as a foreign language with very few points of connections for most students.

Understanding how we process and interpret stories, that is, new knowledge, helps us reflect about our own learning process and make necessary adjustments to improve our learning.

7.8 ANOMALIES OR CONTRADICTIONS CREATED BY THE INPUT STORY

It is also important to consider a series of phenomena that influence our understanding of stories, such as how our brain treats the existence of anomalies, contradictions, and gaps in the input story and other psychological phenomena such as priming and stereotyping. These phenomena are common to all human beings (Quintana, 2017).

Effective metacognitive learners need to constantly check what they understand from the input story by reflecting on their previous stories, knowledge, and experiences, and how they affect their understanding of the input story.

Through the metacognitive process, students need to be aware of their knowledge shortcomings and to be able to act upon them. How can they do so? First, students need to recognize these shortcomings by constantly asking themselves questions about whether what they are learning makes sense, and whether what they know about the input story can be explained through what they already know. If it cannot, because there is a perceived anomaly in the input story or because there is a contradiction between the input story and the activated story (existing cognitive structure), then students need to change what they already know by modifying the activated story. As discussed throughout the book, it will be this need to change the existing story that will lead to the deep learning changes at the individual (brain) and collective levels. Students can do this by reading new material, asking questions, discussing with peers, and writing possible solutions to explain the conflict until they are satisfied that a new modified activated story can explain the input story. For example, suppose that a student erroneously believes that *mens rea* means "intentional mind" and, thus, for this student the only type of *mens rea* is intention. Consistent with this belief, the student further understands that an action carried out with negligence only may not constitute a criminal offence. This is the student's story. Suppose you want that student to learn the concept of *mens rea* and its four main categories (intention, knowledge, recklessness, and negligence). You present the student with a situation (input story) where the perpetrator commits the crime of negligent homicide and is convicted and sentenced to the maximum sentence for this crime. The student, provided he is motivated to grapple with this case, will experience a contradiction between his own story (cognitive structure) and the input story. Research shows that human beings tend to dismiss the input story when it does not fit with their existing stories, or they simply look for the first story which may superficially reconcile both. In this case, the student may either ignore the input story of negligent homicide by not engaging in its discussion or simply believe that the input story is a hypothetical and that negligent homicide is not considered a crime in any real jurisdiction. If students are aware of these cognitive mechanisms, they should constantly check to see if they can keep looking for better stories to solve the conflict presented by the input story. They can do this after a thorough reflective process that includes oral and written self-reflection, discussion with peers, reading of new materials, and any other actions that will result in changing their existing story to best resolve the contradiction and incorporate the input story within their cognitive structure. Remember Ms. Horrible Harriet Hare's students and the blaming of Tiny Tessie. They believed the first explanation about crime responsibility. They did not care to look for other, better explanations.

7.8.1 GAPS CREATED IN THE INPUT STORY

Another related phenomenon that is worth bearing in mind in any meta-cognitive reflective process is the phenomenon whereby people tend to fill gaps that exist in the input story with parts of other stories that they have already incorporated to their cognitive structure. In other words, people complete the information that they receive with what is already in their minds in order to tell a story that is compatible with their life stories (Schank, 2000). For example, in many movies, we see a couple kissing in the bedroom and then there is a cut to that couple naked in bed, looking quite satisfied. The movie does not show us that the couple has had sex, but we complement that story in our minds by including events, emotions, and data that are part of our cognitive structure. Jurors and legal professionals alike do the same with legal stories. If a witness testifies that she saw the accused pull the trigger of a gun and then saw the victim dead on the floor and covered with blood, the witness will complement the witnessed events with information in her knowledge structure and will conclude that the accused actually killed the victim, even if the witness did not see the bullet from the accused's gun penetrate the victim's body. The witness will probably testify that she saw the accused shoot the victim to death. She will not realize that her mind is filling in gaps with actions that she did not see. The process of filling in gaps also occurs when we listen to a story and not only when we see a story.

This is a phenomenon that occurs at a subconscious level. It is a normal and not a pathological phenomenon. In fact, it is a very useful mental resource that helps us understand gaps in input stories. Imagine if we did not have this mental capacity. It would not be possible to carry out even the most trivial tasks such as crossing the street. If we were about to cross the street without traffic lights and we saw a car coming at 100 miles per hour a few feet from the intersection, we could not anticipate that if we crossed the streets the car would run over us. However, this phenomenon can also lead to faulty conclusions. It is possible that the couple did not have sex. It is possible that they simply lay in bed talking about their feelings without having had sex. It is also possible that the accused shot but missed and that someone else (maybe someone hiding near the victim) actually killed the victim.

This phenomenon also happens with knowledge when someone tries to learn something new in an educational setting. For example, suppose that students discuss an input story (whether it is a judicial case, a popular culture text, a news article, or a hypothetical case you make up) about the arrest of the perpetrator of a bank robbery. This story mentions that the perpetrator has a criminal record, including a life imprisonment sentence for murder three decades ago. Suppose that students do not know that life imprisonment in the jurisdiction where this person was tried includes the eligibility for parole after 25 years. So, if the story does not say so explicitly, students will unconsciously perceive that there is a gap in the input story, which they will try to fill in with information that will give coherence to the input story. Again, they will not try to change their existing story. So, some students may believe that the perpetrator escaped prison while serving his prison sentence and was arrested again after the bank robbery. Others, if for example they come from a European country that does not have an equivalent of the confrontation clause, may believe that he was tried in absentia for the murder.

Knowledge of this mental phenomenon helps students realize that they need to constantly check to see if they have filled gaps in the input story with inaccurate information. We can help students by designing metacognitive tools that include specific questions about this phenomenon.

7.8.2 PRIMING

As part of their metacognitive reflection, students should be aware of other phenomena that may—unconsciously—cloud their thinking process. These include priming and various forms of stereotyping.

Priming takes place when an individual receives a stimulus that influences his or her actions in response to a similar stimulus that the same individual receives later. As a way of illustration, suppose a person in Michigan's Upper Peninsula is shown a slice of a dulce de leche cheesecake—a dessert that is not at all popular in Northern Michigan—and that, unlike restaurants in regions with a large Latino population, probably no restaurant offers it in its menu. Then, that person is asked to make a list of desserts one may find in restaurants. This person will likely include dulce de leche cheesecake in his or her answers. If this person has not been primed with dulce de leche cheesecake, he or she may not have thought of this dessert. Similarly, if students discuss a series of input stories dealing with legislative intent as the interpretative method for statutes, and then they are presented with a case that calls for the plain meaning rule, some students will apply the legislative intent method, even if this is incorrect.

Priming can have long-lasting effects, particularly when it is done subliminally. Paul Kolers (1976), an American psychologist with the University of Toronto, conducted a very interesting project in the 1970's to test the effects of priming. He asked university students to read some pages written in upside-down typography. He told the students that they had to read out loud for speed and accuracy. More than a year later, he gave those same students more pages to read in this format. He included a few of the pages that students had read the year before. He measured the speed of their reading. Students read those few pages that they had read before considerably faster than the new pages. Studies in memory and learning confirm that the higher speed may not be attributed to memory, but only to a lasting effect of priming.

In another experiment, four researches—from Stanford University, UCLA, Virginia, and Brooklyn College—exposed undergraduate students to subliminal priming associated with intelligence (Lowery et al., 2008). While working on a seemingly unrelated task, two groups of students were exposed to words that appeared in a computer such as "intelligent, smart, brilliant, bright, talented, sharp, clever, brainy, gifted, educated, genius, and learned" (Lowery et al., 2008). One group of students was told that the activity they did was intended to improve their academic performance. The researchers did not tell anything to the second group. Results in an immediate practice test and the later exam show that students who did not know about the priming performed better than students who knew about the priming experiment.

In the examples reported in the literature, researchers consciously manipulate concepts and explicitly prime their subjects. But priming can also occur unintentionally. We can all prime our students in our classes, even if we do not intend to affect their performances. For example, if we mention a few cases dealing with crimes whose social harm may be committed with wrongful conduct and then we ask our students to give examples of crimes, most will likely give examples of offenses that have the same structure, that is to say, wrongful conduct rather than attendant circumstances or wrongful result. Similarly, if we start a class talking about the final exam, grades, or other issues that may cause student anxiety, when students are asked to conduct an activity—even one that they normally find pleasant—they will unconsciously associate it with the final exam and grades, and they will not enjoy it (Aronson, et al., 2002).

7.8.3   STEREOTYPING

Stereotyping, which is closely connected to priming, may also affect the thinking process. In Chapter 4, I discussed the concept and effects of stereotype threats. Other forms of—overt and deep seated—stereotyping may also negatively impact our thinking and decision-making processes. There are certain groups of people, situations, and traditions that are negatively associated with societal stereotypes.

The criminal justice systems in North America and elsewhere are replete with examples of unfair arrests, prosecutions, convictions, sentencing, and even executions directly linked to stereotyping and discrimination of minorities. A quick examination of the list of death penalty executions in the United States shows that most cases are directly or indirectly linked to stereotyping, which shows its powerful influence.

The impact of stereotyping and discrimination has long entered the university and law school classrooms. This affects students' thinking process and may lead them to incorrect results. Suppose, for, example, that a group of students are given an input story about a bar fight between a white corporate executive man wearing an expensive Armani suit and a visibly drunk, black parolee man wearing baggy jeans and a torn T-shirt. If students are asked to play the role of a police officer who has to figure out what happened and has to act accordingly, including making an arrest if appropriate, most students will probably fill the gap in the input story through the stereotype that poor, drunk, black men are violent. They will most likely conclude that the black man with a criminal record assaulted the white, rich, executive.

7.8.4   THE MERE EXPOSURE EFFECT

When you like something or someone, you are more likely to attribute positive characteristics to them. Liking a person, thing, place, or event has a positive impact on your—unconscious—thought and decision-making processes. A judge who likes the defendant is more likely to—unconsciously—give that person a lighter sentence than to defendant he or she does not like. A job hiring committee will hire a candidate that it likes over a candidate it does not. A teacher is more likely to give a better grade to a student he or she likes.

People get to like the things, events, societies, and places that they are exposed to, provided they do not experience negative effects. Similarly, we like those people whose life stories fit within ours, that is to say, when we find some similarities between their life stories and ours. The popular culture industry knows this very well. When audiences are exposed to celebrities for a long time, celebrities become familiar. They are part of the viewer's everyday life, much like their family and friends. In some cases, viewers can know—or think they know—celebrities better than their own friends. "The mere exposure and familiarity with [the celebrities] leads to positive affect" (Hogarth, 2003). Advertising agencies cast celebrities to make commercials because of what their life stories represent in consumers' minds. For example, Penélope Cruz personifies the ideals of beauty, intelligence, and sophistication that so many people all over the world identify with. Similarly, Beyoncé appeals to audiences because she embodies an image of hard work, honesty, and authenticity.

The flip side of the mere exposure effect is that we tend to dislike the people, events, and things we are not familiar with. This explains factors such as discrimination against people from other backgrounds. In the nutrition realm, research experiments show that children need to be offered a new food between 10 and 15 times before they like it (Lerner and Parlakian, 2007). So, the mere exposure effect can have negative consequences when we have to assess people or things. This lack of familiarity may lead us to erroneous conclusions. For example, in a job hiring process, a hiring committee may erroneously believe that a person whose background they are unfamiliar with or whose life story does not fit with the life stories of the members of the hiring committee is not suitable for the job when in fact the candidate really is. Similarly, a judge or jury may find someone liable or guilty simply because their—unconscious—rapid cognitive models are telling them that they do not like the defendant.

7.9 SUMMARY

Metacognition is the practice of reflecting about and monitoring one's own learning process. It is a very useful strategy that permits the learner to make adjustments and implement changes while learning. Metacognition requires students to be familiar with both general and discipline-specific tools and resources to focus on their learning process. An effective way to present these tools and resources to students is through a series of questions that they can ask while learning law and criminal justice. Students also need to know the mechanisms that our brain uses to interpret and process stories. Equally important, they need to be aware of unconscious mechanisms that affect the understanding of stories. These include priming, stereotyping, the mere exposure effect, and mental methods to deal with anomalies, contradictions, and gaps in the input story.

The next chapter examines an experience in a criminal law course taught entirely through the popular culture.

KEYWORDS

- **metacognition**
- **metacognitive questions**
- **story processing**
- **gaps in input story**
- **priming**
- **stereotyping**

PART 3

Teaching Through Popular Culture

From Vision to Analysis: Teaching a Course on Criminal Law Through Popular Culture Stories

And Slippin' Jimmy I can handle just fine,
but Slippin' Jimmy with a law degree is
like a chimp with a machine gun!
The law is sacred! If you abuse that power, people get hurt!
This is not a game! And you have to know that on some level.

Better Call Saul (Schnauz, 2015).

ABSTRACT

A course that examines criminal law deeply through popular culture stories used as sources for the analysis and discussion of substantive concepts, principles, and theories leads to the creation of a deep learning environment when all the elements of the deep learning process are present in the course. These elements are challenging input popular culture stories, student intrinsic motivation, the creation of a cognitive conflict, connections between the input stories and their existing stories, the use of a wide array of cognitive skills and competences, including rapid cognition, and metacognitive reflection, and the development of media literacy skills.

8.1 INTRODUCTION

In this chapter, I recount an experience in teaching a course on criminal law and popular culture[1]. I begin by briefly exploring Shulman's five-tiered

---

[1]Some events, products, and circumstances were altered in order to protect the identity of the students and the anonymity of their performances.

conception of teaching process: vision, design, enactment, outcomes, and analysis, which serves as the theoretical framework for the analysis of the course. Then, I examine each step of the course following the elements of the teaching process. The selected theme for the course was the abuse and violence against women and children, which offers students an opportunity to interrogate and challenge criminal law and its approach to these phenomena. The intention of the course was to help students examine criminal law deeply through popular culture stories. Popular culture stories are used as sources for the analysis and discussion of criminal law topics. The course also aimed to foster media literacy skills in the criminal law field.

8.2   SHULMAN'S CONCEPTION OF THE TEACHING PROCESS

Shulman (2004) recognizes that teaching is a process that goes beyond the classroom and involves the following stages: (1) vision, (2) design, (3) enactment, (4) outcomes, and (5) analysis. A course usually starts with the exploration of a problem or with an idea or theme that the teacher wants to explore with his or her students. This process involves an inquiry into the overarching problems and themes of the discipline (Blythe, 1998). It continues with the planning of the course. The design phase includes the preparation of the syllabus, the teaching and learning activities that will help students achieve the main goals, and the resources to help students throughout their learning process. Then, the teacher engages with students in the enactment of the course. Shulman (2004) compares the design of the course to a research proposal and the enactment to the process of carrying out research work according to the designed research proposal. The enactment is followed by the achievement of outcomes which are the products of student learning, that is, some changes in the way students think, act, and feel about the issues they dealt with in the course (Bain, 2004). For Shulman (2004), this is equivalent to the results of a research project. Finally, teaching a course entails an analysis of the whole teaching and learning process. The teacher needs to formulate interpretations of the process and its outcomes in light of the vision that originated the teaching enterprise. Shulman (2004) proposes connecting these interpretations to the scholarly community's understanding of the issues and problems that were part of the course. Also, the analysis includes reflection about changes that may need to be adopted to improve the course in the future.

These stages are not strictly linear. Each step feeds the others, and progress in one step frequently requires revisiting other steps. For example, a teacher may have a clear vision of what he or she wants to do in a course. But once he or she starts working in the design, that vision may be reformulated. Similarly, the analysis of the course may lead to changes in the design and enactment of the course the next time it is taught.

8.3   CONTEXT

This course is inserted in a legal studies program at an undergraduate university. The legal studies program is a 4-year program within a social sciences division. Unlike law school programs, which focus on the analysis of legal rules to prepare graduates for the future professional practice of law, the general aim of its program is the same as that of liberal arts education: to foster a general understanding of culture, history, society, sciences, and social organization. This is done by considering law as a social phenomenon and as a social institution, by seeing its connections with culture and society in all aspects and dimensions, and by connecting legal theory with humanities and social sciences. A more specific goal of the program is the critical assessment of the law in different legal traditions and cultures (Sarat, 1999). The program approaches law and legal scholarship as an autonomous discipline, but it also gives ample room to the interdisciplinary perspectives on law that come from the social sciences. The study of law is broad both in its historical and spatial dimensions. It is not limited to the here and now, as occurs in law schools, which implies restricting the study of the law to the current law of the jurisdiction where the law school is situated.

A total of 22 students registered for, and successfully completed, the course. Most students were in the 20–25 age range. Gender was equally represented. 15% of the students were international—two from Africa and one from Eastern Europe. A handful of students were college transfers. Most were first-generation students.

8.4   VISION

My intention with respect to this course was to teach criminal law through the analysis of popular culture stories. I wanted students to have the opportunity to use popular culture stories as the main source of input for their engagement in the examination of criminal law and to produce popular culture texts on criminal law.

This presented several challenges. The first one was that students had taken several courses in criminal law throughout their program—many even with me. I had also taught them many aspects of law and popular culture in several courses, including one on law and films. So, the only possibility to run this course was to find a theme or a coherent series of criminal law topics that they had not analyzed in depth and to find a popular culture angle from which to address these topics.

With respect to the first challenge, I thought of topics and issues that I had wanted to explore in other criminal law courses but which I had to leave off from the course syllabi because of lack of time. The topics that came to my mind were property crimes, child prostitution, terrorism, domestic violence, identity theft, and cybercrimes, among others. These topics are very interesting, and at different points in their majors, students had asked me to discuss them in various courses. All of these issues fit perfectly well within the general description of the special topics course that the university senate had approved. However, I wanted my students to go deeper than simply discuss topics in a senior-year course. So, I decided that we would use criminal law topics as an opportunity to explore and question the fundamental fabrics of criminal law. I must admit that at the time of envisioning the course I did not know exactly how we could connect the selected topics to the critical evaluation of criminal law, but I was confident that I would come up with appropriate ideas while doing research for the preparation of the course.

My broad initial vision needed to be narrowed down and become more specific. I had to start working on the design of the course in order to have a clearer idea of how to translate this broad vision into a more concrete one. Like for a research design in which doing the literature review gives you ideas on how to develop your thesis, exploring popular culture stories would help me define and implement a new vision for the course.

8.5 DESIGN

I decided to poll the students who would take the course about their interests in a course for the following term. I told them that I was developing the course and that I wanted to have their input as the content of the course they wanted to take. I prepared a survey where students had to rank their preferences among different issues and topics of criminal law. Students could also add other topics not suggested among the options. The survey was voluntary and anonymous. 100% of my students, who were taking another course with me, answered it, including a few students who were not registered for my next term's course. These were students who had completed all their fourth-year requirements in the major and who needed to take electives outside the major. Most students wanted a course on criminal law and violence and abuse against women and children. I thought that this was an appropriate and interesting topic, so I decided I would teach a course on this topic.

The second step was to compile a filmography list with films and TV shows from the Internet Movie Database (IMDb) and other resources that I could use as input stories in class. I did not want to include only films and shows whose main theme is domestic violence and which have an explicit criminal law content. I also wanted to include films and shows that deal with other issues but which show elements of violence and abuse against women and children. This is so because in real-life problems of violence and abuse are mixed with other issues. So, I did not necessarily choose courtroom dramas and police detective stories.

Since violence against women and children is a very broad phenomenon, I broke it down into five subtopics that I wanted students to deal with in class: general issues and problems with the legal treatment of violence against women, child exploitation, infanticide, child abuse and neglect, bigamy and polygamy, and violence against women at the hands of the criminal justice system. I also included a category dealing with the comparison between the legal treatment of sexual abuse and property crimes.

I started exploring films and TV shows and classified them according to these categories. I then selected one film or TV (or a series of short clips from TV shows or films) per category.

Copyright is always an issue when you want to show movies and TV shows in class. My university subscribes to several organizations that license films and TV shows for screening in class. I checked the databases of these companies, and all of the films and TV shows that I had selected were covered by the licenses. My university also subscribed to organizations that provide licenses for using and copying articles and books for class use. Because the materials that I would show in class were included in the databases and covered by express copyright agreements, I did not need to consider fair dealing and fair use issues.

8.6   NEW VISION

My objective was to use the theme of abuse and violence against women and children as an opportunity to question and challenge criminal law itself and its approach to dealing with these issues. I needed to come back to my design and formulate a very clear vision for the course in the form of questions which students could find easy to understand. Thus, my vision for the course would be that students could explore the following questions deeply: (1) Is criminal law an adequate approach to deal with abuse and violence against women and children? (2) What are the aspects, premises, philosophy, and structures of criminal law that make it adequate/ inadequate to deal with these issues? (3) What role, if any, plays popular culture in contributing to an increasing reliance on criminal law to deal with these issues?

This vision would guide the enactment of the course, its subsequent student outcomes, and my course analysis. For this purpose, I would construct appropriate instruments—class activities, evaluation tools, and research questions to help students realize this vision and to determine if this vision is materialized.

8.7   THE PROMISING SYLLABUS

My next step was to prepare a course outline. I decided to adopt and implement the promising syllabus. The promising syllabus is a concept developed by Ken Bain (2004). It recognizes that people learn best and most deeply when they have a strong sense of control over their own education rather than feeling manipulated by someone else's demands. The promising syllabus usually contains three components. First, it offers an explanation of the course's promise to the students, i.e., what they will have gained, in terms of knowledge or skills, by the end of the semester. The focus moves away from what the teacher will cover to what the students will take away from the course. Second, it describes the activities in which the students will engage in order to help them fulfill that promise:

the readings, the class activities, and the assignments. Third, the promising syllabus "begins a conversation about how the teacher and the student would best come to understand the nature and progress of the student's learning" (Bain, 2004).

My promise to my students was that if they engaged in the course they would have a deep understanding of the criminal law approach to violence against women and children and the role that popular culture plays in shaping this approach. These were also my learning outcomes. I also promised them that I would do my best to make the course as intellectually challenging and as entertaining as possible, as this fosters intrinsic motivation.

8.8   THE SOLO TAXONOMY

John Biggs developed the Structure of the Observed Learning Outcome or SOLO taxonomy to assess the quality of student learning outcomes (Biggs and Tang, 2007). This taxonomy is divided into five levels, which include lack of understanding (prestructural), a very basic understanding of only a few aspects of a problem, question, or situation (unistructural), an understanding of several but unrelated aspects (multistructural), then an integrated understanding of several aspects into a whole (relational), and finally, the ability to generalize that whole and apply to new situations (extended abstract). Since, pursuant to my university policy, I am required to segment learning and offer more than one evaluation instance in all courses, including a final evaluation, I decided to divide the assessment in five parts, even if I do not believe in fragmenting knowledge and assessment. So, I would assess how well students achieved the intended learning outcomes through their active class participation, which was worth 30% of the final grade, an in-class test worth 20%, a portfolio, worth 10%, a paper worth 15%, and the final global-take home evaluation, which was worth 25% of the final grade. I implemented SOLO taxonomy evaluation criteria for each level of understanding for each of these evaluation components (see Appendix).

8.9   THE BIBLIOGRAPHY

A very important aspect of the syllabus was the required and recommended bibliography. There is no textbook or book that deals with criminal law and popular culture with a focus on violence and abuse against women and children. So, I had to compile the reading list. I wanted to include academic legal texts dealing with violence against women and children. I included an article entitled "Violence Against Women and Children: Some Legal Issues" by Cynthia L. Chewter (2003). The article does not focus exclusively on criminal law issues and does not exhaust the topic, but I thought it was very clearly written and students would get the big picture of the legal problems associated with abuse and violence. So I decided to include this article.

Sheehy (1999)'s article on "Legal Responses to Violence Against Women in Canada" provides a very good feminist theoretical framework written in a language that is accessible for undergraduate students. I have also included articles on bigamy (Bala, 2009; Drummond, 2009), infanticide (Anand, 2010; Osborne, 1987), and child abuse (Poulin, 2003; CCRC, 2011).

8.10 ENACTMENT: STRUCTURE OF THE CLASSES

Every class had a similar structure. It started with an input story: a popular culture story that contained a motivating problem, question, or situation about violence against women and/or children for students to solve, answer, or deal with. For this purpose, students had to work in small groups organized according to diversity parameters. Most of these activities were designed in the spirit of problem-based learning. Problem-based learning is a process where groups of students work with authentic—or simulated—problems (Barrows and *Wee Keng* Neo, 2007). I conceive the notion of the problem in problem-based learning in a very broad sense. A problem is not an equation for students to come up with the right answer or a case for students to decide whether the accused is guilty or innocent. A problem may deal with the analysis of a situation, the discussion of a challenging question, the resolution of a challenge, conflict, or dilemma, or the completion of a project[2]. In their attempt to deal with these problems, students engage in a process of discovery and creation of knowledge. They apply what they already know to the analysis and solution of the problem.

---

[2]Similarly, the solution to the problem is also conceived in a broad sense and it may include students' analysis of a situation, the production of a media text, or the writing of a document used in the legal and criminal justice professions.

Students seek, acquire, and use a wide array of resources. They do research, discuss their findings, and learn about issues that are needed to solve the problem. Students also immerse themselves in discussions about solutions to the problem with their group members. Then, they determine a solution and communicate it to the rest of the class. The rest of the class gives them feedback, which the students may incorporate into a revised solution of the problem (Barrows and *Wee Keng* Neo, 2007).

For some classes, I also prepared guiding questions to help students reflect about the problems, readings, and popular culture texts. Guiding questions orient students' discussions and analysis and help them discover, negotiate, and construct knowledge without transmitting information or imposing any conditions on their learning process. Students were free to focus on some of these questions, disregard others, and even come up with their own questions.

Given the nature of the activities that included the analysis and production of popular culture texts, the class followed an intensive teaching format. It met once a week for 3 h instead of the traditional 90 min twice a week. Although I wanted an even more intensive format with more contact hours, I was only able to negotiate this schedule.

8.10.1   *FIRST CLASS: INTRODUCTION*

The objective of the first class was twofold: to introduce the course and to discuss general aspects of spousal and partner abuse against women (Table 8.1). With respect to the first objective, I wanted students to know what we would be doing throughout the course. So, I introduced the general theme, content, methodology, and evaluation of the course. I also wanted to set a positive environment and to create an enjoyable atmosphere.

With respect to the second objective, I wanted students to reflect about the causes and characteristics of spousal and partner abuse and its legal treatment and to create a website with information and resources for victims. For the input story, I showed the selected scenes of *Law and Order: Criminal Intent, A Murderer Among US* (Shill, 2006). In order to facilitate their analysis, I gave my students some guiding questions. These questions had to do with the analysis of the scene, including rapid cognition strategies and decisions followed by law enforcement agents, and some general questions about violence against women and criminal law.

TABLE 8.1 Violence against Women: Guiding Questions.

- Why does abuse against women happen? Why do some men abuse their wives/ girlfriends/partners? Is it prevalent in our city? Why is it difficult for some women to leave their abusive husbands?

- Why do some abused women believe the abuse is their fault? Why do some victims of sexual abuse feel ashamed?

- What can be done to stop violence against women?

- What is the legal treatment to deal with violence against women? What do you think of the current legal treatment? Should there be a specific crime? If so, how could it be defined? What changes, if any, would you make to Canadian criminal law to better deal with abuse and violence against women?

I also asked them the questions that I would like them to be able to answer deeply by the end of the course. I would ask students these same questions toward the middle of the course and, again, at the end to see if they changed their minds, that is, if the course helped them change the way they view criminal law and its approach to violence against women and children.

These questions included the following:

(i)   Is criminal law and adequate approach to deal with abuse and violence against women and children?

(ii) What are the aspects, premises, philosophy, and structures of criminal law that make it adequate/inadequate to deal with these issues?

(iii) What role, if any, plays popular culture in contributing to an increasing reliance on criminal law to deal with these issues?

Finally, I introduced metacognition tools to help students reflect about their learning process in the course and to be able to monitor this process. This included both criminal law and popular culture metacognitive tools.

8.10.2   SECOND AND THIRD CLASSES: VIOLENCE AGAINST WOMEN

I wanted students to continue developing an understanding of the causes of violence against women and to critically examine the legal treatment of gender violence. Additionally, I wanted students to be able to present their analysis and their findings through a short documentary.

For the input story, I showed scenes from the film A Reason to Believe (Tirola, 1995). I also provided students with some statistics, not because I was interested in the quantitative aspects of the problem, but because I thought that this could give some students an idea of the prevalence of this problem. Students had to produce a documentary on violence against women. For this purpose, they had to examine and deconstruct the conventions of documentary films. Students watched other documentaries and read articles dealing with the narrative structure and the elements used in documentaries, particularly those with a legal focus.

Students also had to examine the international legal framework and the implementation of this framework in Canadian law. I also suggested that they explore the website *Project Stand: Faces of Rape and Sexual Abuse Survivors* designed by Nobuko Oyabu. Additionally, students had to read articles and websites on the causes of violence against women.

8.10.3   FOURTH AND FIFTH CLASSES: CHILD EXPLOITATION

The objective of these classes was to analyze the general international and national legal framework dealing with child exploitation, child prostitution, and child sex trade, including the Canadian and US extraterritorial jurisdiction on child sex trade. I wanted students to recognize those situations where the existing legal treatment appears to be excessive or disproportionate to deal with situations that can better be addressed outside the sphere of criminal law. I also wanted students to be able to apply their knowledge to the making of a victim impact statement video.

The input story included scenes from *Heading South* (Cantet, 2005) and a request to prepare a victim impact statement video. Students had to pretend that Brenda is tried and convicted for having sex with a minor in Haiti. Students had to produce a day in the life of video or a progressive video for a victim impact statement, showing how the repeated sexual intercourse with a forty-something woman affected the child. The video is to be shown in Brenda's hypothetical sentencing hearing. Students had to analyze the harm that this caused the minor and the legal responses to protect him and to convict Brenda and all those responsible for his sexual exploitation. Students had to predict the rapid cognition reactions of the judge, prosecutor, other criminal justice officers, and the victim present in the sentencing hearing. In order to predict these reactions, students were given biographies of all these individuals.

I provided students with guiding questions on the film and the legal aspects of child prostitution and child sex tourism.

TABLE 8.2   Legal Aspects of Sex Tourism: Guiding Questions.

- Why is there child prostitution? Is there child prostitution in our city?
- Why do some children become prostitutes?
- Should there be different criminal offences for child and adult prostitution?
- What can be done to prevent child prostitution?
- What role do drugs play in child prostitution?
- What is the connection, if any, between child molestation and child prostitution?
- What do you think about child sex tourism? What about adult sex tourism?
- Should North American and Western European countries continue to criminalize conducts that take place outside their territories?
- Who should be considered legally responsible for sex tourism?
- Should other countries criminalize conducts in Canada that are against their laws?
- How can sex tourism be prevented? What legal and nonlegal measures could be taken?
- Why do some countries encourage sex tourism?

8.10.4   SIXTH CLASS: INFANTICIDE

The objective of this class was to examine the legal treatment of infanticide and the legal response to the problems associated with post-partum depression. Students had to design a public awareness campaign to reform infanticide law and to implement a similar law as the US Mothers Act in Canada, taking into account the characteristics of the Canadian public health system and their differences with the US system. The campaign had to include appearances in talk shows. For the input story, I asked students to read an article about post-partum depression and its possible connection to infanticide from a lifestyle magazine.

I provided students with guiding questions to examine the legal framework of infanticide and its connection to postpartum depression. Students also had to watch a video about the passage of the Mothers Act, a federal US law encouraging research, education, screening, and treatment of postpartum depression.

TABLE 8.3   Postpartum Depression and Infanticide: Guiding Questions.

Postpartum depression

- What is depression? What does depression feel like? What are the symptoms? What are signs of depression?
- Is depression something you can just 'get over'? Is it a medical issue or just sad thoughts?
- Is depression prevalent among university students? Why or why not? What is the connection, if any, between nutrition and depression?
- Why does postpartum depression occur? Is it a disease?
- Is postpartum depression dangerous for the baby? For the mother? For others?
- Has anyone (or anyone you know) ever experienced postpartum depression or the baby blues? What was it like?
- Do you think postpartum depression may affect men? Why or why not?
- The role of a spouse is crucial for someone experiencing postpartum depression. What about women/men who are single parents?

Legal framework

- Do you agree with the legal treatment given in Canadian criminal law to mothers who kill their babies while suffering from postpartum depression?
- Do a web search of the risk factors associated with postpartum depression. What are the main risk factors? Is violence against women a risk factor?
- Does infanticide occur in nonhuman species? If so, is this relevant for the criminal law treatment of human infanticide? Why or why not? Do a quick search of infanticide in primates. What lessons, if any, can be learned that could be applicable to human beings?
- What are the advantages and disadvantages of the US Mothers Act?
- Should Canada also adopt the Mothers Act? Or a modified version of the Mothers Act? Why? Why not? If so, what changes, if any, would you make to the Mothers Act?

Infanticide and abortion

- Is there a connection between abortion and infanticide? Since abortion is mainly legal in Canada, should infanticide be decriminalized too?
- In an article entitled "After-Birth Abortion: Why Should the Baby Live?" Giubilini and Minerva (2012) claim that "abortion is largely accepted even for reasons that do not have anything to do with the fetus' health. By showing that (1) both fetuses and newborns do not have the same moral status as actual persons, (2) the fact that both are potential persons is morally irrelevant, and (3) adoption is not always in the best interest of actual people, the authors argue that what we call 'after-birth abortion' (killing a newborn) should be permissible in all the cases where abortion is, including cases where the newborn is not disabled." Do you agree with these arguments? Why? Why not?
- Peter Singer (1993), a well-known professor of Bioethics at Princeton University, argues that "killing a newborn baby is never equivalent to killing a person, that is, a being who wants to go on living." How does Singer justify this view? What are his arguments? What connection does he make between abortion and infanticide?

8.10.5   SEVENTH CLASS: ACADEMIC WRITING

The objective of the class was to help students improve their academic writing skills. This is an ongoing objective that cuts across most courses in the program. For consistency with program outcomes and curriculum, I had to include a class devoted to this objective. I was afraid some students would find this a boring and would react negatively; as they tend to believe that they already write well and that they do not have to learn how to write.

Students learn how to write in the same way they learn other competences, skills, and practices. But, writing—like many other complex processes—presents also some specific issues that need to be taken into account. In order to learn how to master disciplinary writing deeply, students need to be faced with an input story that contains a story conflict that their current disciplinary literacy level is not sufficient to solve. In this case, writing itself must be the problem and the new knowledge arising from the input story should be a different writing style (or a higher level of writing) that students have not yet mastered. Like with any learning, students need to be motivated to do make—nonarbitrary and substantive—connections between the new writing genre or style and their current writing style through the use of higher order cognitive and metacognitive skills, processes, practices, and competences.

So, I presented students with the challenge of having to answer questions from victims of gender violence, most of whom asked about legal information and resources in the community. Whereas most students were quite proficient in writing academic essays, they faced the challenge of writing legal issues clearly at a level to be understood by diverse group of women, including some without formal education and some whose first language was not English. The input story was the victims' stories that they told students while asking them questions. At first, most students answered their questions in a way their readers did not understand. This became apparent in the follow-up questions that victims asked. In general, they repeated their questions because they did not understand their answers. For their new answers, students dissected the readers' writing style and adapted their own to their readers' writing, which proved successful. While we started this practice on Class 7, it continued for the rest of the semester. Some students even continued after the course ended.

Toward the end of class seven, I also asked students to write the answers of the same questions I asked them on the first class. I wanted students to be aware of how their initial thoughts changed halfway through the course. I provided students with guiding questions to and showed them a video of professional screenwriters' discussion of their writing style.

TABLE 8.4   Academic Writing Metacognitive and Guiding Questions.

•   Discuss and describe your experience in writing essays.
•   Is learning to write in the legal disciplines at the undergraduate level important? Do you think you will use these skills after you finish your undergraduate studies?
•   What are the major obstacles you face when writing an essay? What type of feedback helps you? What doesn't help you?
•   Discuss the expert writing process according to Bean (2011). What can you do to follow this process for your own essay in this course?
•   Do you follow the 5-essay paragraph to write about law? Why or why not?
•   Do you rewrite? Why or why not? How often? What do you change when you rewrite?
•   What does legal research mean? How do you do research from a legal positivist perspective?
•   Analyze the structure of a standard law review article according to Gerald Lebovits (1996).
•   What is a claim according to Eugene Volokh (2010)? Think of and write, at least, one example of a prescriptive claim, a descriptive claim, and a claim which includes a combination of both.
•   Discuss some selected screenwriters' approaches to writing. What do you find useful for legal writing from these approaches?

8.10.6   EIGHTH CLASS: COMPARISON OF THE LEGAL TREATMENT OF OFFENCES DEALING WITH DOMESTIC VIOLENCE AND ABUSE AND PROPERTY CRIMES

The objective of this class was to encourage students to compare the legal treatment of property offences and offences involving domestic violence and abuse. The input story consisted of a series of clips showing property crimes, including scenes from *Friends*' episodes *The One with all the Cheesecakes* (Halvorson, S 7, E 11, 2001) and *The One Where Rosita Dies* (Prime, S7, E 13, 2001), *Seinfeld's* episode *The Limo* (Cherone, S 3, E 1992), and *Pink Panther's Slink Pink* (Pratt, 1969), among many others. Students had to produce a radio call-in show discussing the similarities and differences of the legal treatment of property crimes and domestic violence and abuse. The radio show had to include the interview of a criminal defense attorney and a police officer. In one of these interviews, the radio show host had to read some hypothetical situations dealing with property and sexual assault offences for the interviewee to give his or her rapid cognition reactions to those situations.

In order to prepare for the radio show, students had to discuss offences dealing with property rights, their definitional terms, the existence of presumptions, such as the doctrine of recent possession, and the adoption of specific offences to protect property rights. In the radio talk show, some students had to assume the role of the host and other students had to play the role of defense lawyers, legislators, police officers, and judges (Quintana, 2018).

8.10.7   NINTH AND TENTH CLASSES: CHILD ABUSE AND NEGLECT

The objective of these classes was to analyze the international, national, and provincial treatment of child abuse and child neglect. I wanted students to recognize the different situations that constitute abuse and neglect and to identify the existing gaps in the legal framework to adequately deal with these situations.

The input story included selected scenes from the films *Hotel for Dogs* (Freudenthal, 2009). Students had to choose one child from the film and produce a sentencing mitigating video for the parents or caregivers of a neglected or abused child found guilty in a hypothetical trial of that parent or caregiver. In preparation for the sentencing mitigating videos, students had to discuss the legal framework at the international, national, and provincial levels. Students also had to watch sentencing videos and read articles written by legal scholars and practitioners that discussed the film and legal conventions of sentencing mitigating videos.

8.10.8   ELEVENTH CLASS: BIGAMY AND POLYGAMY

This class dealt with bigamy, polygamy, and other crimes against conjugal rights. The objective was to analyze the legal framework in Canada and to compare it with the legal treatment in other states. Students had to produce the pilot for a TV show on bigamy. The story had to revolve around a man married to two women at the same time, and it had to include a criminal trial. The pilot also had to include scenes of criminal justice officers using rapid cognition strategies to solve legal and criminal problems. The input story included a clip from the film *The Bigamist* (Lupino, 1953). It tells the story of a married man who lives a double life in San Francisco and Los Angeles.

TABLE 8.5   Bigamy and Polygamy: Guiding Questions.

(1)	What are some of the reasons for criminalizing bigamy and polygamy?
(2)	Do you agree with criminalizing bigamy in our present society? Why or why not?
(3)	Who practices polygamy? Why?
(4)	BC Chief Justice held that "women in polygamous relationships are at an elevated risk of physical and psychological harm. They face higher rates of domestic violence and abuse, including sexual abuse." Are these valid reasons to criminalize polygamy?
(5)	Why is polygamy a crime when three consenting adults agree to live together in a conjugal union? What are the advantages, if any, of polygamy?
(6)	Do you agree with the criminalization of polygamy? Why or why not?
(7)	What Charter rights, if any, may be infringed by the criminalization of polygamy and bigamy?
(8)	What are some of the causes of adultery? What are some of the consequences of adultery?
(9)	Do you agree with the legal treatment of adultery in Canada? Do you think it should be criminalized?
(10)	What messages do we get from society and media about adultery?

8.10.9   TWELFTH AND THIRTEENTH CLASSES: CRIMINAL JUSTICE AND VIOLENCE AGAINST WOMEN

These were the last substantive classes. They dealt with women as perpetrators of crimes and the abuse that many suffer at the hands of the criminal justice system. Students also had to look for a wrongfully convicted female and do research about her case. Then, they had to produce a clemency video to request her exoneration. For the input story, I asked students to read the play *The Exonerated* by Jessica Blank and Erik Jensen (2004) and to analyze it from a legal perspective.

TABLE 8.6   Exoneration: Guiding Questions.

- What is exoneration? Is there compensation for wrongful convictions in the United States? What about Canada?
- Who is Sonia "Sunny" Jacobs? What happened to her? Why was she convicted? What happened to her husband? How was Sunny finally released? What did she do when she was released? Why wasn't Sunny Jacobs released immediately after Walter Rhodes' confession?
- Who is Jesse Tafero? What is his story?
- Who is Walter Rhodes? What is his story? What do you think about the plea bargain? Analyze it critically. What are the pros and cons of plea bargains? What are the usual consequences and implications of plea bargaining?
- Who is Peter Pringle? What is his story?
- Does the death penalty really deter crime?
- What is the history of the death penalty in Canada and its abolition?
- What does the American Convention of Human Rights (known as the Pact of San Jose) say about the death penalty? Is Canada a party to this treaty? Why or why not?
- Sister Helen Prejean (1994), author of *Dead Man Walking*, argues that "All of us are worth more than our worst act." What does this mean? Do you agree? Why or why not?

8.10.10   FINAL CLASS: EVALUATION

The final evaluation was instrumented as a take-home exam. Students had to complete three questions, activities, or problems. The first question was mandatory for all students. Then students could choose two questions from the remaining alternatives.

The first question dealt with the connection between criminal law and popular culture. I included the same questions as the ones that I had asked students at the beginning and middle of the course. I asked them to have a new look at these questions and to reflect on whether and, if so how, the course changed their original answers.

Another question asked students to write a script for a documentary based on one or more of the stories from Sin by Silence, Women Against Abuse, or a similar website.

Students had to produce a sentencing mitigating video for Ricardo Morales in The Secret in their Eyes (Campanella, 2009). Morales has kept Gomez imprisoned for 25 years. Gomez had raped and killed Morales' wife. Students were given a summary of the transcripts of a hypothetical trial against Ricardo Morales. They also had to predict the rapid cognition reactions from the judge, the prosecutor, and the victim. In order to predict their reactions, students received a short biography of all these individuals and examples of previous intuitive reactions in different settings.

In another question, I asked students to watch and analyze the film *A Reason to Believe* (Tirola, 1995), which narrates a campus rape after a fraternity party. I wanted students to analyze the incident and to explore the reasons why it happened. Students had to produce a TV talk show focused on their analysis.

The last question asked students to make a documentary about a wrongfully convicted female based on the film Double Jeopardy (Beresford, 1999).

8.11 OUTCOMES AND ANALYSIS

Students' performance on the final evaluation showed that they reflected quite seriously about the inadequacy of criminal law to deal with domestic violence. Most focused their analysis on the postintervention approach of criminal law, its punitive nature, and its rigidity and formalities to deal with a very sensitive and complex social issue. All students were able to identify the role of popular culture and the increasing societal reliance on criminal law to deal with abuse and violence against women and children.

The analysis of students' evaluations and performances throughout the course clearly indicates that practically every single student has achieved instances of deep learning. This is evidenced by the high quality of the teaching and learning activities that included the analysis of challenging issues of violence against women and children as well as the production of media texts on these issues that were evaluated following John Biggs' SOLO taxonomy.

It is not easy to compare the outcomes of a course with those of another course. There are many variables that may influence student learning from one semester to another even when you try to control as many variables as possible. Still, the comparison of the same questionnaire and essay written by students in this course and the ones written by other students who took a similar course that did not include the popular culture aspect shows that students who took the criminal law and popular culture course achieved a deeper understanding of the same topics than students who took a more traditional course.

Students' perception of their learning—obtained through anonymous end-of-course surveys—was also very favorable. A very strong majority of students agreed and strongly agreed that studying criminal law through popular culture helps understand criminal law. Most also found the popular culture approach to be interesting. A strong majority also found that the course adequately covered all relevant criminal law aspects of domestic violence. Similarly, most students felt that they had a good knowledge of criminal law aspects of domestic violence.

The average grade for this course was 80.65. The grade average in a course on criminal law taught the previous semester under the same or similar conditions, except for the popular culture perspective, was 74.81.

The triangulation of these data supports the conclusion that a criminal law course taught through popular culture stories and aimed at fostering the development of media literacy is conducive to the creation of a deep learning environment.

TABLE 8.7   Course Feedback Questions.

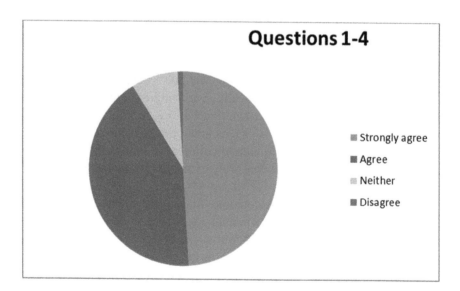

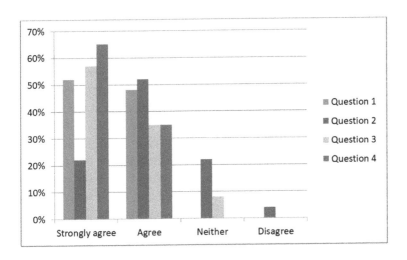

TABLE 8.8   Survey Analysis.

Survey analysis

- Question 1: Studying criminal law through popular culture helps understand criminal law:
  - o   Strongly agree: 12 (52%)
  - o   Agree: 11 (48%)
- Question 2: Studying criminal law through popular culture is interesting.
  - o   Strongly agree: 5 (22%)
  - o   Agree: 12 (52%)
  - o   Neither agree nor disagree: 5 (22%)
  - o   Disagree: 1 (4%)
- Question 3: The course adequately covered all relevant criminal law aspects of domestic violence.
  - o   Strongly agree: 13 (57%)
  - o   Agree: 8 (35%)
  - o   Neither agree nor disagree: 2 (8%)
- Question 4: I now have a good knowledge of criminal law aspects of domestic violence.
  - o   Strongly agree: 15 (65%)
  - o   Agree: 8 (35%)

8.12 SUMMARY

Teaching a course on criminal law and popular culture can lead to the creation of a deep learning environment when all the elements of the deep learning process are present. These include interesting input popular culture stories that embed a problem, question, or situation for students to grapple with (Bain, 2004) and that create a cognitive conflict while students make connections between the input stories and their existing stories, the use of these popular culture stories as sources for the analysis and discussion of criminal law topics, the promotion of student intrinsic motivation, and the fostering of a wide array of cognitive skills and competences, including rapid cognition, and metacognitive reflection (Hermida, 2015).

Shulman's five-tiered conception of the teaching process helps examine the development of the course from vision to analysis (Shulman, 2004). The recounted experience focused on abuse and violence against women and children. It aimed to encourage students to question criminal law and its treatment of violence against women and children at the international and national levels. It also aimed to promote the development of media literacy skills, including both the interpretation and production of popular culture stories in the criminal law realm.

Students' attainment of learning outcomes proved to be of higher quality than the achievement of learning outcomes in a similar course taught without recourse to popular culture stories.

KEYWORDS

- course design
- promising syllabus
- SOLO taxonomy
- teaching process
- learning outcomes
- academic writing
- writing styles
- literacy levels

CHAPTER 9

Conclusions

ABSTRACT

Teaching for deep learning is the answer to the superficial quality of learning that takes place in traditional law school and criminal justice classrooms. Deep learning is a committed approach to learning where learners learn for life and can transfer and apply what they learn to different situations and contexts in their personal, social, and professional lives. Teaching for deep learning entails creating a safe and motivating environment, where the learner interacts with an exciting input story that contains a problem, question, or situation within the learner's zone of proximal development. This gives rise to a cognitive conflict, derived from the learner's social interaction with peers. If motivated enough, the learner will use higher-order cognitive skills, competences, and processes (individually and together with peers) to make connections between an activated story in the learner's existing cognitive structure and the new knowledge in the input story. As a result, the learner will change his or her cognitive structure (conceptual change) and will move from a community of knowledge to another or toward the center of an academic or professional community.

9.1 ACCEPTED

In *Accepted* (Pink, 2006), Bartleby Gaines is a senior high school student. He is the typical slacker. He never studies. He is not interesting in learning anything. He cannot articulate his thoughts clearly. He is incapable of helping others learn. He is not engaged in any extracurricular activities. Nor does he do any volunteer work in the community. He spends most of his time partying, drinking, and hanging out with friends. He does not have a clue what he wants to do in life.

Bartleby applies to eight colleges. Not surprisingly, every single one turns him down. He becomes frustrated and desperate. He does not want to let his parents down, so he creates his own college: South Harmon Institute of Technology. He asks a friend to create the college website, and he rents an abandoned psychiatric hospital to build the college campus. He has no intention to learn. The college is only a façade so that his parents will not bother him. To his surprise, some of his friends and hundreds of other students from all over the country, who have also been rejected by other colleges, show up to attend South Harmon Institute of Technology.

Bartleby faces a situation for the first time in his life. He is aware that hundreds of students depend upon him to learn. He understands that he has to do something to turn South Harmon Institute of Technology into a real college. He understands that he has to create an environment that helps him and others learn for real.

He compares and contrasts what is going on at South Harmon Institute of Technology with his own experiences in high school. He talks to his closest friends who are attending his college. He also goes to Harmon College, a prestigious higher education institution in the same city, to tour the campus. He talks to some students and staff there. Back at South Harmon, Bartleby discusses what he has seen at Harmon College with his closest friends. Gradually, he begins to change his attitude and approach to learning.

As a result of these—individual and collective—reflections and interactions, Bartleby encourages all students to reflect about what they want to learn and to write their answers on a big wall. This becomes the curriculum. Some students are interested in learning how to cook; others are interested in digital photography. Other students are merely interested in swimming or riding bikes over a swimming pool. Bartleby does not repress any of these goals. On the contrary, he encourages them to pursue their dreams and provides all students with the resources so that they can engage in a process of deep learning. Students create their own classes. There are no textbooks, grades, essays, required readings, or courses. The students are the teachers. They reflect and work collaboratively, and they give each other feedback constantly.

When South Harmon Institute of Technology's future is jeopardized, because the dean of Harmon College files a complaint with the accrediting agency, Bartleby comes to its rescue. He articulates his case very persuasively. He explains the teaching philosophy and the curriculum to the agency. He gives evidence of having met every requirement for obtaining accreditation. He is also quick to address all the concerns and challenges that the complainant raises. It is clear that Bartleby has learned deeply to reflect about his actions, to argue, and most important, to create an environment that encourages himself and others to learn deeply.

9.2 TEACHING LAW AND CRIMINAL JUSTICE THROUGH POPULAR CULTURE

The pedagogies that predominate in law schools and in university criminal justice programs have given rise to a culture of surface learning. These pedagogies include the case-dialogue method in US law schools, the seminar in most criminal justice graduate programs, and the lecture in undergraduate criminal justice university programs in North America and Europe as well as in European and Canadian faculties of law. These teaching methods have several factors in common: the limelight is on the teacher, who controls the pedagogical aspects of the class, either by trans-mitting information, asking questions or by organizing student exchanges. The teacher also formulates the learning goals, performs in class, and evaluates students. Students lack the possibility of engaging in profes-sional and academic performances in authentic—or recreated—settings, and they lack the opportunity to discover and construct knowledge by themselves and with peers.

Teaching for deep learning is the answer to the superficial quality of learning that takes place in traditional law school and criminal justice classrooms. Deep learning is a committed approach to learning where learners learn for life and can transfer and apply what they learn to different situations and contexts in their personal, social, and professional lives. Teaching for deep learning entails creating a safe and motivating environment, where the learner interacts with an exciting input story that contains a problem, question, or situation within the learner's zone of proximal development. This gives rise to a cognitive conflict, derived from the learner's social interaction with peers. If motivated enough, the learner will use higher order cognitive skills, competences, and processes (individually and together with peers) to make connections between an activated story in the learner's existing cognitive structure and the new knowledge in the input story. As a result, the learner will change his or her cognitive structure (conceptual change) and will move from a community of knowledge to another or toward the center of an academic or professional community. In *Accepted* (2006), Bartleby changes the way he thinks about education and the way he interacts with other students. He stops drinking, partying, and procrastinating. Instead, he shows a strong desire to learn and a genuine interest in helping all students learn. At the same time, Bartleby gradually leaves the community of slacker students to join the community of deep learners and educators.

Teaching for deep learning also entails fostering and facilitating a process of evaluation and metacognitive reflection about the whole learning process, including individual and collective changes. Metacognition is the practice of reflecting about, and monitoring, one's own learning process through a series of general and discipline-specific tools. It also entails an awareness of the way the deep learning process functions and the unconscious mechanisms that affect this process such as priming, stereotyping, the mere exposure effect, and mental methods to deal with anomalies, contradictions, and gaps in the input story.

When the elements of the deep learning environment are not present, learning is merely superficial. Students tend to forget what they learn in class as soon as they finish their courses and are unable to apply what they learn in new contexts.

Popular culture, which is pervasive in today's society and includes all cultural texts, such as films, TV shows, songs, books, magazines, plays, radio shows, and commercials, among many others, helps enhance and maximize the whole deep learning process. It provides pedagogically rich input stories that create cognitive conflicts and help activate the learner's repertoire of existing cognitive stories. It is also a very useful tool to reflect about substantive aspects of the legal and criminal justice disciplines. Popular culture also promotes the development of cognitive skills that are difficult to acquire in traditional law school and university classrooms, such as rapid cognition thought processes. Rapid cognition, a strategy widely used in the legal and criminal justice professions, consists of the fast processing of stimuli and information that leads to intuitive conclusions and decisions. Popular culture offers countless possibilities to help students fully develop their rapid cognition skills and to reflect upon them.

Popular culture, together with the absence of negative and harmful factors, such as a stressful classroom atmosphere, discrimination, and stereotyping, also contributes to—intrinsically—motivate students to engage in the deep learning process. At the same time, it helps students find pleasure in their learning endeavors. Popular culture texts dealing with legal and criminal justice themes also contribute to recreate professional settings where students can engage in professional activities in the classroom.

Popular culture stories have greatly influenced and shaped the legal and criminal justice professional fields. They affect virtually every aspect of professional practice: from police interaction with suspects and victims to lawyers' performance in the courtroom.

Popular culture stories share their narrative structure with the stories told in the legal and criminal justice disciplines. Academic disciplines narrate several stories: a general story that is common to all their members and a series of specific stories that those members produce in their everyday professional or academic practice. Law tells the story of the regulation of human behavior through laws enforced objectively by judges. Criminal justice tells the story of a system and its agents (police, courts, and prisons) that deal with crime in order to protect individuals and society.

With the advent of the revolution in media and global communications in the last few decades, lawyers and criminal justice officers are increasingly becoming producers of popular culture and other media texts in their daily professional practice. Despite the significance of popular culture and media texts in the legal and criminal justice professions, law and criminal justice teachers do not equip their students with the tools to interpret and produce legal popular culture and other media texts. Similarly, teachers do not use popular culture texts as primary sources for the study of law or criminal justice.

Teaching a course that relies on popular culture to provide input stories and that aims to promote the development of media literacy skills, including both the interpretation and production of popular culture stories and other media texts, can create an environment conducive to student deep learning. This requires the presence of all elements of the deep learning process: exciting input stories that embed a problem, question, or situation for students to deal with, the creation of a cognitive conflict, opportunities for meaningful interaction with peers, the encouragement of students to make connections between the input stories and their existing stories, the fostering of student use of higher order cognitive skills, competences, and practices individually and collectively, including rapid cognition, the promotion of student intrinsic motivation, and a climate of permanent metacognitive reflection.

KEYWORDS

- **deep learning**
- **popular culture**
- **law and popular culture**
- **criminal justice**

References

Aguayo, A. *Documentary and Social Change: A Rhetorical Investigation of Dissent.* Unpublished doctoral dissertation; University of Texas, Austin, USA, 2005.

Alsultany, E. Why Stereotypes, 2013; http://www.arabstereotypes.org/why-stereotypes.

Anand, S. Rationalizing Infanticide: A Medico-Legal Assessment of the Criminal Code's Child Homicide Offence. *Alberta L. Rev.* **2010,** *47,* 705–728.

Argyris, C. *On Organizational Learning;* Blackwell; Cambridge, MA, 1993.

Argyris, C.; Schön, D. *Theory in Practice;* Jossey-Bass, San Francisco, 1974.

Aronson, J.; Fried, C.; Good, C. Reducing the Effects of Stereotype Threat on African American College Students by Shaping Theories of Intelligence. *J. Exp. Soc. Psychol.* **2002,** *38,* 113–125.

Asimow, M.; Mader, S. *Law and Popular Culture;* Peter Lang Publishing, New York, 2004.

Ausubel, D. P.; Novak, J. D.; Hanesian, H. *Educational Psychology: A Cognitive View;* Holt, Rinehart and Winston, New York, 1978.

Bain, K. *What the Best College Teachers Do;* Harvard University Press, Cambridge, MA, 2004.

Bain, K. *What the Best College Students Do;* The Belknap Press of Harvard University Press, Cambridge, MA, 2012.

Bala, N. Why Canada's Prohibition of Polygamy is Constitutionally Valid and Sound Social Policy. *Can. J. Fam. L.* **2009,** *25,* 165–221.

Barrows, H. S.; Wee Keng Neo, L. *Principles and Practice of a PBL;* Pearson Prentice Hall, Singapore, 2007.

Beale, S. The News Media's Influence on Criminal Justice Policy: How Market-Driven News Promotes Punitiveness. *William Mary L. Rev.* **2006,** *48,* 2.

Bean, J. *Engaging Ideas: The Professor's Guide to Integrating Writing, Critical Thinking, and Active Learning in the Classroom;* Jossey-Bass, San Francisco, 2013.

Bennett, T. Popular Culture: A Teaching Object. *Screen Education* **1980,** *34,* 17–30.

Berman, S. H. Gone But Not Forgotten; Script Unpublished, 2005.

Biggs, J.; Tang, C. Teaching for Quality Learning at University, 4th ed.; McGraw-Hill, Society for Research into Higher Education; Open University Press, Maidenhead, 2011.

Blank, J.; Jensen, E. *The Exonerated;* Faber and Faber, Inc., New York, 2004.

Brinkley, A.; Dessants, B.; Flamm, M.; Fleming, C.; Forcey, C.; Rotschild, E. *The Chicago Handbook for Teachers. A Practical Guide to the College Classroom, Chicago;* The University of Chicago Press, Chicago, 2011.

Canadian Coalition for the Rights of Children. Working Document: Violence against Children, Research Report, 2011; http://rightsofchildren.ca/wp-content/uploads/Working-Document-Violence-Against-Children-Research-Report-update-Sept-2011.pdf

Casper Martinez, S. Utilizing the Tools: Successfully Implementing the Stalking Statutes. *Land Water L. Rev.* **2000,** *35,* 521–524.

Cassuto, L. Student-Centered Graduate Teaching. *The Chronicle of Higher Education*, November 4, 2013.

Chewter, C. L. Violence against Women and Children: Some Legal Issues. *Can. J. Fam. L.* **2003**, *20*, 99–178.

Clark, L. M. G. Feminist Perspectives on Violence against Women and Children: Psychological, Social Service, and Criminal Justice Concerns. *Can. J. Women L.* **1989–1990**, *3*, 420.

Cotter, C. *News Talk: Investigating the Language of Journalism*; Cambridge University Press, Cambridge, 2010.

D'Amato, A. *Jurisprudence: A Descriptive and Normative Analysis of Law*; Martinus Nijhoff, Dordrecht, 11984.

Dammeyer, M. M.; Nunez, N. Anxiety and Depression among Law Students: Current Knowledge and Future Directions. *L. Human Behav.* **1999**, *23*, 55.

Dowler, K.; Fleming, T.; Muzzatti, S. L. Constructing Crime: Media, Crime, and Popular Culture. *Can. J. Criminol. Crim. Just.* **2006**, *48*, 6.

Drummond, S. G. Polygamy's Inscrutable Criminal Mischief. *Osgoode Hall L. J.* **2009**, *47*, 317–369.

Duncum, P. Toward a Playful Pedagogy: Popular Culture and the Pleasures of Transgression. *Stud. Art Educ.* **2009**, *50* (3), 232–244.

Giroux, H. A.; Simon, R. I. Schooling, Popular Culture, and a Pedagogy of Possibility. *J. Educ.* **1988**, *70* (1), 9–26.

Giubilini, A.; Minerva, F. After-Birth Abortion: Why Should the Baby Live? *J. Med. Ethics* **2012**; doi:10.1136/medethics-2011-100411.

Gladwell, M. *Blink. The Power of Thinking without Thinking*; Back Bay Books, New York, 2005.

Goldfarb, B. *Visual Pedagogy: Media Cultures in and beyond the Classroom*; Duke University Press, Durham, NC, 2002.

Gramsci, A. *The Antonio Gramsci Reader: Selected Writings 1916–1935*; New York University Press, New York, 2000.

Gregson, C. B. California's Antistalking Statute: The Pivotal Role of Intent. *Golden Gate Univ. L. Rev.* **1998**, *28*, 221.

Grimm, J.; Grimm, W. *Grimms' Household Tales, Vol. 1*; George Bell and Sons; London, 1884.

Guskin, H. *How to Stop Acting*; Faber and Faber, New York, 2003.

Handelsman, J.; Miller, S.; Pfund, C. *Scientific Teaching*; Freeman, New York, 2007.

Harmer, J. *The Practice of English Language Teaching*; Longman Press, Essex, 2001.

Hatchett, F.; Gitlin, N. *Frank Hatchett's Jazz Dance*; Human Kinetics: Champaign, IL, 2000.

Hatfield, E.; Cacioppo, J. T.; Rapson, R. L. Emotional Contagion. In *Review of Personality and Social Psychology*; Clark, M. S., Ed., Vol. 14; Sage: Newbury Park, CA, 1992.

Herman, J. H.; Nilson, L. B. *Creating Engaging Discussions: Strategies for "Avoiding Crickets" in Any Size Classroom and Online*. Styles; Stylus, Sterling, VA, 2018.

Hermida, J. Teaching Criminal Law in a Visually and Technology Oriented Culture: A Visual Pedagogy Approach. *Leg. Educ. Rev.* **2006**, *16*, 14–26.

Hermida, J. *Facilitating Deep Learning: Pathways to Success for University and College Teachers*; Apple Academic Press (Taylor & Francis), Boca Raton; Oakville, 2015.

Hermida, J. *Canadian Criminal Law*; Wolters Kluwer Law and Business, Alphen aan den Rijn, The Netherlands, 2018.

Hirsch, E. D. *Cultural Literacy: What Every American Needs to Know*; Houghton Mifflin, Boston, 1987.

Hobbs, R. The Seven Great Debates in the Media Literacy Movement. *J. Commun.* **1998,** *48*, 16.

Hogarth, R. M. Educating Intuition: A Challenge for the 21st Century. *Els Opuscles del CREI* **2003,** *13*.

Jameson, F. *Postmodernism, or the Cultural Logic of Late Capitalism*; Duke University Press, Durham, NC, 1991.

Kahneman, D. *Thinking Fast and Slow*; Doubleday Canada, Toronto, 2011.

Keller, D. New Technologies/New Literacies: Reconstructing Education for the New Millennium. *Teach. Educ.* **2000,** *11* (3), 246.

Kolers, P. A. Reading a Year Later. *J. Exp. Psychol.* **1976,** *2*(5), 554–565.

Krashen, S. D. The Case for Narrow Reading. *Lang. Mag.* **2000,** *3*(5), 17–19.

Krech, D.; Rosenzweig, M. R. The effects of an Enriched Environment on the Rat Cerebral Cortex. *J. Comp. Neurol.* **1964,** *123*, 111–119.

Lacy, D. Print, Television, Computers, and English. *ADE Bulletin 072*, 1982; http://www.adfl.org/ade/bulletin/n072/072034.htm.

Lambert, N. M.; Stillman, T. F.; Fincham, F. D.; Baumeister, R. F.; Hicks, J. A. To Belong Is to Matter: Sense of Belonging Enhances Meaning in Life. *Personal. Soc. Psychol. Bull.* **2012,** *39* (11), 1418–1427.

Lang, J. M. *Small Teaching: Everyday Lessons from the Science of Teaching*; Jossey-Bass, San Francisco, 2016.

Le Brun, M.; Johnstone, R. *The Quiet (R)evolution: Improving Student Learning in Law*; Law Book Co, Sydney, 1994.

Lebovits, G. The Legal Writer. Academic Legal Writing: How to Write and Publish. *NYSBA* **2006,** *64*, 50–54.

Lepper, M. R.; Greene, D.; Nisbett, R. E. Undermining Children's Intrinsic Interest with Extrinsic Reward: A Test of the "overjustification" Hypothesis. *J. Personal. Soc. Psychol.* **1973,** *28* (1), 129–137.

Lerner, C.; Parlakian, R. *Healthy from the Start: How Feeding Nurtures Your Young Child's Body, Heart, and Mind*; Zero to Three, Washington, DC, 2007.

Lowery, B. S.; Eisenberger, N. I.; Hardin, C. D.; Sinclair, S. Long-term Effects of Subliminal Priming on Academic Performance. *Basic Appl. Soc. Psychol.* **2007,** *29* (2), 151–157.

MacArthy, T. F. *MacArthy on Cross Examination*; American Bar Association, Chicago, 2007.

MacFarlane, J. A Feminist Perspective on Experience-Based Learning and Curriculum Changes. *Ottawa L. Rev.* **1994,** *26*, 357, 383.

Malla, P. Shantytown; Book Review; The Globe and Mail, 2013.

McNutt, R.; Wright, P. C. Coaching Your Employees: Applying Sports Analogies to Business. *Exec. Dev.* **1995,** *8* (1), 27–32.

Miller, N. *The Poetics of Gender*; Columbia University Press, New York, 1986.

Morrell, E. Toward a Critical Pedagogy of Popular Culture: Literacy Development among Urban Youth. *J. Adol. Adult Lit.* **2002,** *46*, 1.

Mottet, T. P.; Beebe, S. A. Emotional Contagion in the Classroom: An Examination of How Teacher and Student Emotions Are Related. *Annual Meeting of the National Communication Association, 86.*

Mutz, D. C.; Nir, L. Not Necessarily the News: Does Fictional Television Influence Real-world Policy Preferences? *Mass Commun. Soc.* **2010,** *13* (2), 196–217.

Osborne, J. A. The Crime of Infanticide: Throwing Out the Baby with the Bathwater. *Can. J. Fam. L.* **1987,** *6,* 47–59.

Owens, E. G. *Media and the Criminal Justice System.* Cornell University, Ithaca, NY, 2009.

Oyabu, N. Project Stand: Faces of Rape and Sexual Abuse Survivors; http://nobukoonline.com.

Perkins, D. *Making Learning Whole. How Seven Principles of Teaching Can Transform Education*; Jossey-Bass, San Francisco, 2009.

Perry, S. The Law According to Seinfeld: Using a Show about Nothing to Teach Law. *The 48th Annu. MBAA Int. Conf.*; Chicago, March 28–30, 2012.

Pink, D. H. *Drive. The Surprising Truth About What Motivates Us*; Riverhead Books, New York, 2009.

Poulin, R. Globalization and the Sex Trade: Trafficking and the Commodification of Women and Children. *Can. Woman Stud.* **2003,** *22* (3/4), 38.

Prejean, H. *Dead Man Walking. The Eyewitness Account of the Death Penalty That Sparked a National Debate*; First Vintage Books; New York, 1994.

Quintana, L. Character: Anticathexis and Ego Alteration. In *Proceedings of the X Research Conference*. Faculty of Psychology, UCES, Buenos Aires, 2015a.

Quintana, L. Feminine Character and Masculinity Complex. In *Proceedings of the VII International Congress of Research and Professional Practice*; Faculty of Psychology, University of Buenos Aires, Buenos Aires, 2015b; pp 536–538.

Quintana, L. Character and Trauma. In *Proceedings of the VI International Congress of Research in Psychology*; National University of La Plata, La Plata; pp 625–630.

Quintana, L. Defence: Character and Break. In *Proceedings of the X International Congress of Research and Professional Practice*; Faculty of Psychology, University of Buenos Aires, Buenos Aires; pp 620–623.

Quintana, L.; Hermida, J. The Hermeneutics Methods and Research in Social Sciences. *Contrib. L.* **2019,** *3,* 1–16.

Rochette, A. *Teaching and Learning in Canadian Legal Education: An Empirical Exploration.* Unpublished doctoral dissertation; McGill University, Montreal, Canada, 2011.

Rosenthal, A. *Re-envisioning Teaching Graduate Seminars*; KU Center for Teaching Excellence, Kansas City, 2005; https://cte.ku.edu/portfolios/rosenthal2005.

Rosenthal, R.; Jacobson, L. *Pygmalion in the Classroom: Teacher Expectation and Pupils' Intellectual Development*; Holt, Rinehart, and Winston; New York, 1968.

Rosenthal, R.; Rabin, D. B. Interpersonal Expectancy Effects: The First 345 Studies. *Behav. Brain Sci.* **1978,** *1,* 377–386.

Ross, A. *No Respect: Intellectuals and Popular Culture*; Routledge, London, 1989.

Ruiz, R. *Poetics of Cinema*; Dis Voir, Paris, 1995.

Sarat, A. *Legal Scholarship in the Liberal Arts*; Cornell University Press, Ithaca, NY and London, 1999.

Schank, R. C. *Explanation Patterns*; Lawrence Erlbaum Associates, Hillside, NJ, 1986.

Schön, D. *The Reflective Practitioner. How Professionals Think in Action*; Temple Smith, London, 1983.

Sheehy, E. Legal Responses to Violence against Women in Canada. *Can. Woman Stud.* **1999,** *19*, 62–73.

Shulman, L. S. *Teaching as Community Property: Essays on Higher Education*; Jossey-Bass, San Francisco, 2004.

Singer, P. *Taking Life: Humans. Practical Ethics*; Cambridge University Press, Cambridge, 1993.

Smith, A. E.; Jussim, L.; Eccles, J. Do Self-fulfilling Prophecies Accumulate, Dissipate, or Remain Stable Over Time? *J. Personal. Soc. Psychol.* **1999,** *77(3)*, 548–565.

Stabile, C.; Ershler, J. *Constructivism Reconsidered in the Age of Social Media: New Directions for Teaching and Learning*; Jossey Bass, San Francisco, 2016.

Stanislavski, C. *An Actor Prepares*; Theatre Arts Books, New York, 1936.

Stein, R. A. The Future of Legal Education. *Minnesota L. Rev.* **1991,** *75, 945, 952.*

Svensson, N. Extraterritorial Accountability: An Assessment of the Effectiveness of Child Sex Tourism Laws. *Loy. L.A Int'L & Comp. L. Rev.* **2006,** *28*, 641.

Tagg, J. *The Learning Paradigm College*; Anker Publishing Company, Bolton, MA, 2003.

Volokh, E. *Academic Legal Writing: Law Review Articles, Student Notes, Seminar Papers, and Getting on Law Review*, 4th ed.; Foundation Press, New York, 2010.

Wagner, A.; Pencak, W. *Images in Law*; Ashgate; Hampshire, 2007.

Warner, L. M. Technocentrism and the Soul of the Common Law Lawyer. *Am. Univ. L. Rev.* **1998,** *48*, 85–85.

Weston, C.; Cranton, P. A. Selecting Instructional Strategies. *J. High. Edu.* **1986,** *57*, 259–262.

Wicker, B.; Keysers, C.; Plailly, J.; Royet, J. P.; Gallese, V.; Rizzolatti, G. Both of Us Disgusted in *My* Insula: The Common Neural Basis of Seeing and Feeling Disgust. *Neuron* **2003,** *40* (3), 655–664.

Winston, P. *How to Speak*; Derek Bok Center for Teaching and Learning, Harvard University, Cambridge, MA, 1997.

Zulawski, Z. E.; Wicklander, D. E. *Practical Aspects of Interview and Interrogation*; CRC Press, Ann Arbor, 1988.

Zull, J. *The Art of Changing the Brain: Enriching the Practice of Teaching by Exploring the Biology of Learning*; Stylus, Sterling, VA, 2002.

Appendix: Course Outline

CRIMINAL LAW AND POPULAR CULTURE

EXPLORATION
(Formerly known as course description)

This course is a rigorous and fascinating exploration of advanced Criminal Law topics. We will focus on the broad theme of violence against women and children. We will examine the Criminal Law treatment of physical, psychological, and sexual abuse of women. We will also explore child prostitution, infanticide and postpartum depression, and other crimes against children. We will also compare the Criminal Law treatment of sexual offences and property crimes to see if our law tends to protect property more than sexual integrity. Finally, we will delve into abuse suffered by women in the hands of the Criminal Justice system. All this will let us examine and question the fabrics of Criminal Law and to construct alternative solutions for problems associated with violence against women and children both within and beyond Criminal Law.

This course is embedded in the nascent field of law and popular culture, which deals with both the role law plays in popular culture and the role popular culture plays in law. The course is also inserted within the Visual Pedagogy movement, which calls for developing media literacy in the classroom.

At the end of the course, you will have a deep understanding of the Criminal Law approach to violence against women and children and the role that popular culture plays in shaping this approach. From my experience teaching similar courses, I can assure that you will never be able to watch Law and Order—or other similar TV shows—in the same way you have so far. I also promise you that I will do my utmost best to make this course as intellectually challenging and as entertaining as possible.

LEARNING OUTCOMES

If you actively engage in this course, upon its successful completion you will be able to:

- demonstrate a deep understanding of the Criminal Law approach to violence against women and children.
- critically analyze complex and contemporary Criminal Law problems dealing with violence against women and children from diverse legal traditions, theoretical perspectives, and Social Science disciplines related to Law.
- generate your own—sophisticated—solutions to Criminal Law problems involving violence against women and children, identify and evaluate the political and social implications of your proposed solutions, and compare these solutions to those offered in other legal traditions and cultures.
- critically examine the role that popular culture plays in shaping the Criminal Law approach to violence against women and children.
- read academic texts on Criminal Law dealing with violence against women and children deeply, and communicate complex arguments on these issues effectively both orally and in writing; and
- make connections to theories, readings, class discussions, and class activities when analyzing complex Criminal Law issues involving violence against women and children, and theorize, generalize, and hypothesize on these issues.

WHAT WE WILL DO IN OUR EXPLORATION

We will immerse in this exploration through popular culture under-stood in a broad sense. We will watch and critically analyze films, TV shows, documentaries, and TV commercials. We will complement all this with court cases, legislation, and academic journal articles on these topics. We will also resort to group discussions, Socratic dialogues, cooperative group problem solving, games, debates, construction of web sites, and interpretation and production of audiovisual materials.

CALENDAR

Class	Topic	Readings
Class 1	Introduction and orientation	Hermida, Julian. Teaching Criminal Law in a Visually and Technology Oriented Culture: A Visual Pedagogy Approach, Legal Education Review, Vol. 16, Nov. 2006.
Class 2	Violence against women Verbal, physical, and sexual abuse Sexual assault and rape Sex offenders' registration No drop policy	Chewter, Cynthia L. "Violence Against Women and Children: Some Legal Issues" (2003) Canadian Journal of Family Law 20, 99-178. Sheehy, Elizabeth, "Legal Responses to Violence Against Women in Canada" (1999) 19 *Canadian Woman Studies* 62-73. Clark, Lorenne M.G. "Feminist Perspectives on Violence against Women and Children: Psychological, Social Service, and Criminal Justice Concerns" (1989-1990). 3 Can. J. Women & L. 420.

Class	Topic	Readings
Class 3	Child prostitution Child sex tourism	Cecil, Jennifer L. Criminal: Enhanced Sentences for Child Prostitution: The Most Hidden Form of Child Abuse. (2005) 36 McGeorge L. Rev. 815. Richard Poulin, "Globalization and the sex trade: trafficking and the commodification of women and children" (2003) *Canadian Woman Studies* 22, No. 3/4 p.38. Svensson, Naomi. "Extraterritorial Accountability: An Assessment of the Effectiveness of Child Sex Tourism Laws." 2006 *Loy. L.A Int'L & Comp. L. Rev* 28:641.
Classes 4 and 5	Post-partum depression. Mothers' Act Infanticide Academic writing (Class 5)	Osborne, Judith A. The Crime of Infanticide: Throwing Out the Baby with the Bathwater" 6 (1987) Canadian Journal of Family Law 47-59. Lebovits, Gerald, The Legal Writer. Academic Legal Writing: How to Write and Publish, 64 NYSBA 2006, 50. Volokh, E. Academic Legal Writing (9-15).
Class 6	Property crimes	Canadian Criminal Code
Class 7	Midterm	
Class 8	Violence against children Child neglect, child abuse, child abandonment Child abduction Amber Alert Bullying	Canadian Coalition for the Rights of Children (2011). Working Document: Violence Against Children, Research Report. Lesley E. Daigle. "Empowering Women to Protect: Improving Intervention with Victims of Domestic Violence in Cases of Child Abuse and Neglect" (1998) 7 Tex. J. Women & L. 287.
Class 9	Bigamy as a form of abuse against women	Drummond, Susan G. "Polygamy's Inscrutable Criminal Mischief" 47 (2009) Osgoode Hall Law Journal pp. 317–369. Bala, Nicholas. "Why Canada's Prohibition of Polygamy is Constitutionally Valid and Sound Social Policy" 25 (2009) Canadian Journal of Family Law pp. 165–221.
Class 10	The Death Penalty and the Exonerated. Wrongful convictions	The Exonerated by Jessica Blank and Erik Blank (excerpts).

Class	Topic	Readings
Class 11	Review	
	Paper	
	Portfolio	
	Distribution of final take-home	
Class 12	SUBMISSION OF FINAL TAKE HOME	

This is a tentative calendar of what we will do. If class discussions or class activities take longer than originally estimated, I will not cut them short to follow this schedule. I will simply put them off for the following class, or I will reschedule them. Additionally, I may substitute new topics for some of the ones included here, particularly if most of you show an interest for some issues not planned to be covered. Changes will be announced in class. Please note that preparation for these activities, as well as the reviews for the evaluations, also constitutes a fundamental part of the course and is considered an integral part of class instruction. When appropriate, in-class time will be used for preparation for activities, assignments, and evaluations.

A CONVERSATION ABOUT YOUR LEARNING AND DISCOVERIES
(Formerly known as method of evaluation)

In our exploration of Criminal Law topics, we will stop several times so that we can talk about your learning. I will be providing you with formative feedback along the way. There will be plenty of opportunities to experiment, try, fail, and receive formative feedback in advance of and separate from summative evaluation. I will also help you develop the metacognitive tools and strategies so that you can assess your own learning progress. By the end of this exploratory process, you will have showed me what you have taken out of it, what you have learned, and how your thinking has changed. I will be particularly interested in seeing how well you have achieved the learning outcomes. I will want to see if you can perform the learning outcomes in a way which shows creativity, originality, and critical thinking skills, ideally beyond information given in the course.

I will assess the evidence you will show me holistically and synoptically. And I will make a judgment about whether you have attained the intended learning outcomes, and if so—to what level. I will assess your evidence qualitatively and in its entirety—not by adding marks to its various parts. I will be interested in knowing how well you have learned and not how much. My judgment—like any judgment or assessment—will be subjective, but let me assure you that it will not be arbitrary. It will be based on my expertise as both a legal scholar and a teacher, not unlike a juror at a film festival judges films or a curator judges pictures for a museum exhibition. For this purpose, I will judge the quality of your learning against criteria based on John Bigg's Solo Taxonomy, which I have posted on the course website, and which I will explain extensively in class. As you can see from the chart below, the SOLO Taxonomy is consistent with the University grading scheme. To communicate my judgment in a clear way, I will resort to several means, including rubrics.

According to University policy requirements, which prescribe a final global examination and some kind of partition of the summative assessment, I have divided the assessment in five parts, even if I do not believe in fragmenting knowledge and assessment. So, I will be assessing how well you have achieved the intended learning outcomes through your active class participation, which is worth 30% of your final grade, an in-class test worth 20% of the final grade, a portfolio, which is worth 10%, a paper worth 15% of the final grade, and the final global-take home evaluation, which is worth 25%. This syllabus includes a chart that translates the SOLO taxonomy levels into grades according to University policy.

SUMMARY OF THE ASSESSMENT

Evaluation tool	Grade weight	Deadline
Class participation	30%	Every class
Classroom test	20%	Class 7
Paper	15%	Class 11

Evaluation tool	Grade weight	Deadline
Portfolio	10%	Class 12 Each class activity must be done in class
Final Global take-home evaluation	25%	Class 12

CLASS PARTICIPATION

Class participation is the single most important aspect of the course. You are expected to actively participate in every class with a positive attitude and to treat your classmates and teacher with respect. You are expected to get actively involved with the class activities, to critically analyze the proposed problems and situations, to actively participate in small group discussions, to contribute your analysis to the whole class, and to complete all reading and written assignments. You will also conduct oral presentations throughout the course. Class participation also entails asking meaningful questions in the lectures, answering questions, and volunteering comments related to the content of the lectures and the class activities. I will also call on you throughout the course to answer questions or to provide your opinion. We will resort to a broad range of class activities. Some will be conducted individually and others in small groups. Each of you is expected to write down your answers to the class activities, even if you work in small groups, and to keep all activities. You also need to keep record of your oral interventions at the small and whole group levels. A reflective journal is an ideal tool to do this. Many class activities will include the writing and editing of short essays. Other activities will deal with projects and audiovisual presentations. You are expected to be prepared for every class, i.e., you need to do the required readings for each class, and to complete the reading guides and other homework assignments, which you must bring to class. You must also bring a printed copy of the class activities or your laptop to class, as well as the textbook, the journal articles, the course outline, record of your oral interventions, and your class notes to work on the class activities. You have to keep all your class activities, together with these materials, in a portfolio. You have to bring the portfolio to every class. You will not be able to participate when you do not bring these materials to class, as you will be unable to work.

Even if you have a laptop, you must also bring a notebook and pens and be prepared to hand in written class assignments to me when required.

On several occasions throughout the course, I will ask you to hand in the class activities or the entire portfolio for me to give you formative feedback. You are required to take the initiative and come to my office during my office hours to discuss your class performance several times throughout the course. Your class participation must reflect that you have done the required readings and that you have thought about what you read. Simply talking in class is not enough to get a good grade under this evaluation component. But, if you do not talk and participate in class, you will not receive any credit at all. Please note that the written assignments and reading quizzes are conceived to help you prepare to talk in class and fully participate in the class activities. **You will not get a passing grade under class participation if you only do the written assignments but do not contribute to class discussions and class activities.** I expect that active class participation will foster, among many other skills, your oral communication and presentation skills. Class attendance is a prerequisite to obtain the corresponding percentage of the grade under this category. I will evaluate your participation every class. If you miss class you will not receive any kind of credit for that missed class regardless of the reason for your absence, even if you decide to complete the written class activity.

Evaluation Criteria for Class Participation

I will assess whether and how well you have achieved the learning outcomes of the course for the class participation component of the grade according to the following five levels of John Bigg's Solo taxonomy.

Prestructural
The student does not participate actively in most classes. The student does not show that he/she has read the assigned texts. The student does not participate in an appropriate manner that contributes to class discussions and does not show a positive attitude toward his or her classmates, the instructor, and the activities. The student does not work in small groups and does not volunteer to lead activities, debates, and debriefs. The student seldom asks questions in class.

The student responses to the class activities contain irrelevant information, and they miss the point. The responses have no logical relationship to the question. The student gives bits of unconnected information, which have no organization, and make no sense. The student does not make connections to the theoretical issues, readings, class discussions, and class activities done throughout the course. The response to the class activities does not show an understanding of the issues dealt with.

Unistructural

The student participates actively in most classes. In most classes, the student shows that he/she has read the assigned texts. The student generally participates in an appropriate manner that contributes to class discussions and shows a positive attitude toward his or her classmates, the instructor, and the activities. The student works in small groups, but does not always volunteer to lead activities, debates, and debriefs. The student sometimes asks useful questions that contribute to the development of the class and fosters collective understanding or usually asks simple questions that do not contribute to the development of the class.

The student responses to the class activities contain one relevant item, but they miss others that might modify or contradict the response. There is a rapid closure that oversimplifies the legal issue or problem. The student makes simple and obvious connections to some of the theoretical issues, readings, class discussions, and class activities done throughout the course, but the significance of the connections is not demonstrated. In most class activities, the student can identify and list the legal issues or questions presented in class. The response to the class activities does not show an understanding of the issues dealt with or it demonstrates only a very superficial understanding.

Multistructural

The student participates actively and meaningfully in most classes. In most classes, the student shows that he/she has read the assigned texts and that he/she has reflected about the required readings. The student participates in an appropriate manner that contributes to class discussions and shows a positive attitude toward his or her classmates, the instructor, and the activities. The student works productively in small groups and volunteers to lead activities, debates, and debriefs on most classes. The student generally asks useful questions that contribute to the development of the class and fosters collective understanding.

The student responses to the class activities contain several relevant items, but only those that are consistent with the chosen conclusion are stated, and the significance of the relationship between connections is not always demonstrated. Closure in the class activities is generally selective and premature. The student makes a number of connections to theoretical issues, readings, class discussions, and class activities done throughout the course, but the meta-connections between them are missed, as is their significance for the whole. In most class activities, the student can enumerate, describe, combine, and list the legal issues or questions presented in class. The student uses some of the relevant data.

Relational

The student participates actively and meaningfully in every class. The student shows every class that he/she has read the assigned texts quite deeply and that he/she has critically reflected about the required readings. The student participates in an appropriate manner that contributes to class discussions and shows a positive attitude toward his or her classmates, the instructor, and the activities. The student works productively in small groups and volunteers to lead activities, debates, and debriefs every class or most classes. The student asks useful questions that contribute to the development of the class and fosters collective understanding.

The student makes connections to theoretical issues, readings, class discussions, and class activities done throughout the course. In general, students demonstrate the relationship between connections and the whole. In every class activity, the student can focus on several relevant aspects, but these aspects are generally considered independently. Response to the class activities is a collection of multiple items that are not always related within the context of the exercise. In all class activities, the student is able to classify, compare, contrast, combine, enumerate, explain causes, and analyze the legal issues or questions presented in class. The student uses most or all of the relevant data, and he/she resolves conflicts by the use of a relating concept that applies to the given context of the question or problem.

Extended Abstract

The student participates actively and meaningfully in every class. The student shows every class that he/she has read the assigned texts deeply and that he/she has critically reflected about the required readings. The student participates in an appropriate manner that contributes to class discussions and shows a positive attitude toward his or her classmates, the instructor, and the activities. The student works productively in small groups and volunteers to lead activities, debates, and debriefs every class. The student asks useful questions that contribute to the development of the class and fosters collective understanding.

The student makes connections not only to theoretical issues, readings, class discussions, and class activities done throughout the course but also to issues, theories, and problems beyond information arising from class. In every class activity, the student shows the capacity to theorize, generalize, hypothesize, and reflect beyond the information given. The student even produces new relevant hypotheses or theories. In every class, the student can link and integrate several parts, such as class activities, readings, class discussions, and theories, into a coherent whole. The student links details to conclusions and shows that he/she understands deeply the meaning of issues and problems under analysis. The student questions basic assumptions, and gives counter examples and new data that did not form part of the original question or problem.

PORTFOLIO

You are expected to create a portfolio to record all class activities while you carry them out in class. Yes, you need to do your portfolio in class. If you miss class you will not receive any kind of credit for that missed class, even if you decide to complete the written class activity. For further clarification, doing the class activities for the portfolio when you missed class or doing them at home when you did not work in class will not be accepted, and they will not be marked for the portfolio component of the evaluation. You are free to create the portfolio as you please. It can be done in electronic format or in paper. The important aspect of the portfolio is that you record all class activities while you do them IN CLASS.

The deadline for the submission of the portfolio is March 26, 2013 in class. However, if you need your portfolio to do the final take-home, you can submit it together with the take-home on April 2, 2013 in class.

Evaluation Criteria for the Portfolio

I will resort to the Solo taxonomy to judge how well you have achieved the learning outcomes in the portfolio.

Prestructural
The student responses to the class activities contain irrelevant information, and they miss the point. The responses have no logical relationship to the question. The student gives bits of unconnected information, which have no organization, and make no sense. The student does not make connections to the theoretical issues, readings, class discussions, and class activities done throughout the course. The response to the class activities does not show an understanding of the issues dealt with.
Class activities are not carried out in class.
Unistructural
The student responses to the class activities contain one relevant item, but they miss others that might modify or contradict the response. There is a rapid closure that oversimplifies the legal issue or problem. The student makes simple and obvious connections to some of the theoretical issues, readings, class discussions, and class activities done throughout the course, but the significance of the connections is not demonstrated. In most class activities, the student can identify and list the legal issues or questions presented in class. The response to the class activities does not show an understanding of the issues dealt with or it demonstrates only a very superficial understanding.

Multistructural

The student responses to the class activities contain several relevant items, but only those that are consistent with the chosen conclusion are stated, and the significance of the relationship between connections is not always demonstrated. Closure in the class activities is generally selective and premature. The student makes a number of connections to theoretical issues, readings, class discussions, and class activities done throughout the course, but the meta-connections between them are missed, as is their significance for the whole. In most class activities, the student can enumerate, describe, combine, and list the legal issues or questions presented in class. The student uses some of the relevant data.

Relational

The student makes connections to theoretical issues, readings, class discussions, and class activities done throughout the course. In general, students demonstrate the relationship between connections and the whole. In every class activity, the student can focus on several relevant aspects, but these aspects are generally considered independently. Response to the class activities is a collection of multiple items that are not always related within the context of the exercise. In all class activities, the student is able to classify, compare, contrast, combine, enumerate, explain causes, and analyze the legal issues or questions presented in class. The student uses most or all of the relevant data, and he/she resolves conflicts by the use of a relating concept that applies to the given context of the question or problem.

Extended Abstract

The student makes connections not only to theoretical issues, readings, class discussions, and class activities done throughout the course but also to issues, theories, and problems beyond information arising from class. In every class activity, the student shows the capacity to theorize, generalize, hypothesize, and reflect beyond the information given. The student even produces new relevant hypotheses or theories. In every class, the student can link and integrate several parts, such as class activities, readings, class discussions, and theories, into a coherent whole. The student links details to conclusions and shows that he/she understands deeply the meaning of issues and problems under analysis. The student questions basic assumptions, and gives counter examples and new data that did not form part of the original question or problem.

CLASSROOM TEST

The classroom test will aim at testing functional knowledge of the problems and issues discussed in class. See the evaluation criteria below.

PAPER

The paper will deal with the theme of violence against women and children. Specific requirements and instructions will be given in class. The paper will elaborate on the theories, methods, and issues analyzed in class. It must make specific reference to debates, class activities, and problems discussed in class. It must also conform to the writing style, conventions, and specifications explained in class. You are expected to research about the topic and to read from several sources for the elaboration of your paper. The writing of the paper is an individual enterprise. The paper must also comply with the following requirements: approximately 2,000 words, correct use of English (spelling, grammar, and clarity), and correct citation according to the Canadian Guide to Uniform Legal citation.

Evaluation Criteria for the Paper

I will resort to the Solo taxonomy to judge how well you have achieved the learning outcomes in the paper.

Prestructural The paper contains irrelevant information, and it misses the point. The paper has no logical relationship to the selected topic. The paper deals with bits of unconnected information. It has no organization, and it makes no sense. The student does not make connections to the theoretical issues, readings, class discussions, and class activities done throughout the course. The paper does not show an understanding of the issues dealt with. The paper does not follow the required writing style.
Unistructural The paper contains one relevant item, but it misses others that might modify or contradict the position taken. There is a rapid closure that oversimplifies the legal issue or problem. The student makes simple and obvious connections to some of the theoretical issues, readings, class discussions, and class activities done throughout the course, but the significance of the connections is not demonstrated. The student can identify and list the legal issues or questions discussed in class. The paper does not show an understanding of the issues dealt with or it demonstrates only a very superficial understanding. The paper minimally follows the required writing style.

Multistructural

The paper contains several relevant items, but only those that are consistent with the chosen position are stated, and the significance of the relationship between connections is not always demonstrated. Closure is generally selective and premature. The student makes a number of connections to theoretical issues, readings, class discussions, and class activities done throughout the course, but the meta-connections between them are missed, as is their significance for the whole. The student enumerates, describes, combines, and lists the legal issues or questions presented in class. The student uses only some of the relevant data in the presentation. The paper follows only some aspects of the required writing style.

Relational

The paper is a collection of multiple items that are not always related within the context of the selected topic. The student classifies, compares, contrasts, combines, enumerates, explains causes, and analyzes the legal issues or questions presented. The student uses most or all of the relevant data, and he/she resolves conflicts by the use of a relating concept that applies to the given context of the selected issue. The student makes connections to theoretical issues, readings, class discussions, and class activities done throughout the course. In general, the paper demonstrates the relationship between connections and the whole. The student focuses on several relevant aspects, but these aspects are generally considered independently. The paper follows most aspects of the required writing style.

Extended Abstract

The paper makes connections not only to theoretical issues, readings, class discussions, and class activities done throughout the course but also to issues, theories, and problems beyond information arising from class. The student shows the capacity to theorize, generalize, hypothesize, and reflect beyond the information given. The student even produces new relevant hypotheses or theories. The student can link and integrate several parts, such as class activities, readings, and theories, into a coherent whole. The student links details to conclusions and shows that he/she understands deeply the meaning of issues and problems under analysis. The student questions basic assumptions, and gives counter examples and new data that did not form part of the original question or problem. The paper follows the required writing style.

FINAL GLOBAL TAKE-HOME EVALUATION

The purpose of the global take-home evaluation is to assess whether and how well you have achieved the intended learning outcomes. The global take-home examination will be distributed and will have to be submitted as determined in the class schedule above.

Evaluation Criteria for the Final Take-Home Evaluation and for the In-Class Test

I will resort to the Solo taxonomy to judge how well you have achieved the learning outcomes in the final take-home evaluation and the in-class test.

Prestructural
The student responses to questions and problems contain irrelevant information and they miss the point. The responses have no logical relationship to the question. The student gives bits of unconnected information, which have no organization, and make no sense. The student does not make connections to the theoretical issues, readings, class discussions, and class activities done throughout the course. The response to the questions and problems does not show an understanding of the issues dealt with.

Unistructural
The student responses to the questions and problems contain one relevant item, but they miss others that might modify or contradict the response. There is a rapid closure that oversimplifies the legal issue or problem. The student makes simple and obvious connections to some of the theoretical issues, readings, class discussions, and class activities done throughout the course, but the significance of the connections is not demonstrated. The student can identify and list the legal issues or questions discussed in class. The responses do not show an understanding of the issues dealt with or it demonstrates only a very superficial understanding.

Multistructural
The student responses to questions and problems contain several relevant items, but only those that are consistent with the chosen conclusion are stated, and the significance of the relationship between connections is not always demonstrated. Closure is generally selective and premature. The student makes a number of connections to theoretical issues, readings, class discussions, and class activities done throughout the course, but the meta-connections between them are missed, as is their significance for the whole. The student can enumerate, describe, combine, and list the legal issues or questions presented in class. The student uses some of the relevant data.

Relational
Response to the questions or problems is a collection of multiple items that are not always related within the context of the exercise. The student is able to classify, compare, contrast, combine, enumerate, explain causes, and analyze the legal issues or questions presented. The student uses most or all of the relevant data, and he/she resolves conflicts by the use of a relating concept that applies to the given context of the question or problem. The student makes connections to theoretical issues, readings, class discussions, and class activities done throughout the course. In general, students demonstrate the relationship between connections and the whole. The student can focus on several relevant aspects, but these aspects are generally considered independently.

> **Extended Abstract**
>
> The student makes connections not only to theoretical issues, readings, class discussions, and class activities done throughout the course but also to issues, theories, and problems beyond information arising from class. The student shows the capacity to theorize, generalize, hypothesize, and reflect beyond the information given. The student even produces new relevant hypotheses or theories. The student can link and integrate several parts, such as class activities, readings, and theories, into a coherent whole. The student links details to conclusions and shows that he/she understands deeply the meaning of issues and problems under analysis. The student questions basic assumptions, and gives counter examples and new data that did not form part of the original question or problem.

CONVERSION OF GRADING SYSTEM

In order to comply with University policy, which we will all abide by, and in order to facilitate the reading of the SOLO taxonomy, the following chart translates the SOLO taxonomy's five levels into the University grading scheme. As you can see, the descriptions of the levels of the SOLO taxonomy and the University grading scheme mean the same, even if they are expressed in different terms.

SOLO taxonomy	Grade	Percentage of grade value	Definition	
Extended abstract	A	80–100	Exceptional performance	Comprehensive knowledge in depth of the principles and materials treated in the course, fluency in communicating that knowledge and originality and independence in applying material and principles.
Relational	B	70–79	Good performance	Thorough understanding of the breadth of materials and principles treated in the course and ability to apply and communicate that understanding effectively.
Multistructural	C	60–69	Satisfactory performance	Basic understanding of the breadth of principles and material treated in the course and an ability to apply and communicate that understanding competently.

SOLO taxonomy	Grade	Percentage of grade value	Definition	
Unistructural	D	50–59	Minimally competent performance	Adequate understanding of most principles and material treated in the course, but significant weakness in some areas and in the ability to apply and communicate that understanding.
Prestructural	F	0–49	Inadequate performance	Inadequate or fragmentary knowledge of the principles and material treated in the course, or failure to complete the work required in the course.

Please note that in many cases, you may perform at a level in some aspects of a certain evaluation component of the course and at a different level in other aspects. In those cases, for the purpose of the summative assessment, I will determine which level is most representative of your learning. Strategic answers and interventions will be considered at the surface level, i.e., unistructural or multistructural.

RESOURCES

You will need to read all the articles listed above deeply. You are responsible to get them from the library databases. You must read these texts and any other text which you may find it necessary to prepare to participate in class.

A website is available. You will be able to explore and consult the course syllabus, the class activities, and other useful information. You must regularly check both the course website and your official university email account.

I am here to guide you all throughout this process of exploration. Think of me as your expedition experienced companion, i.e., someone who has traveled this route several times before but is still amazed at the wonders discovered along the route.

RULES AND POLICIES

This exploration may only be successful if you engage in it, and if you work honestly and enthusiastically. Since this is a collective exploration, you also need to follow certain rules and policies so that the learning process will be fair to all. Here are the rules and policies. They may sound strict. They are. But, trust me, they have been conceived so that this exploration is as smooth and productive as possible.

OFFICE HOURS POLICY

I do hope you will visit during my office hours. Come individually or with friends. It is a chance to get to know each other and to talk about the course, assignments, tests, study strategies, or whatever else you would like to discuss. I am also available to write letters of reference and to help you plan for future graduate studies or a professional career. Also, if you find yourself having difficulty with anything in the course, please do come. But, remember, you do not have to have a problem to visit. If my office hours are impossible for you, please let me know so that we can make an appointment for another time. In addition to regular office hours and seeing me by appointment, I will every so often end class 5 minutes early and invite students who have questions to meet with me right then and there.

WRITTEN ASSIGNMENT POLICY

Unless otherwise authorized by me in writing, all writing assignments must be submitted personally in hard copy IN CLASS on the due date. For further clarification, written assignments submitted to the Faculty Secretaries, left in my mailbox, sent by email, or slid under my office door, will not be accepted for marking, and you will not receive any credit. Unless I have approved an extension in writing, at my discretion, written assignments submitted after the deadline will either not be accepted for marking, or will be accepted for marking with late penalties. Late penalties will be as followed. If the written assignment is submitted the class following the deadline, a 25% late penalty will be deducted from the mark. A 50% late penalty will be applied to those assignments submitted two classes after the deadline, and no mark will be given if submitted after two classes following the deadline. In those exceptional cases where I grant an extension, you will have to submit your assignment personally IN CLASS on the new specified date.

I will return all written assignments as soon as possible given the number of students registered in the course. Whenever feasible, I will try to return tests and other written assignments the class following the scheduled date for the test or the deadline for submission, respectively. You are expected to get the assignments back from me that class. If you did not come to class, you will have to come to my office during my office hours to get your test or written assignment back. I will presume you did not attend class if you did not get your assignment from me when I distributed them. It is your responsibility to keep a backup copy of each assignment that you submit.

UNIVERSITY ATTENDANCE POLICY

The general regulations of the university require punctual and regular attendance at the various academic exercises. If there are extenuating circumstances related to an absence, the instructor should be notified in writing. Absences in excess of 20% may jeopardize receipt of credit for the course. Given the nature of the course, I will strictly enforce this policy.

ATTENDANCE POLICY FOR THIS COURSE

Your presence and participation in every class are an essential part of the learning process for you and your classmates. Therefore, attendance will be taken at all classes and is mandatory. I will take attendance in a variety of ways, including, sign-up sheets, submission of written activities, and return of assignments. I may also simply write down the names of those students that I noticed that were absent. Arriving late or leaving early without a proper justification will count as an absence. Forgetting to sign the attendance sheet will constitute an absence. Students that have an absence in more than 20% of the classes will NOT receive credit for this course regardless of the reason for the absence, including, without limitation, absences due to medical reasons, sports competitions, and employment obligations. If you missed classes because you were not registered in the course, those classes that you missed will count as absences in order to calculate this 20% rule. This is because I firmly believe that the class constitutes a unique learning environment and most of what you will learn takes place in class, not in solitude. So missing classes—for whatever reason—will hurt your scholastic performance. For further clarification, participation in sports competitions does not exempt you from attending class or for complying with other course requirements. If your sports activities prevent you from regularly attending class, please consider dropping this course as your grade may be seriously affected. Again, this is so because the course is conceived so that you will learn collaboratively with your colleagues and with my guidance. As a matter of courtesy, I may permit a student athlete to write a test on a different day if there is a conflict with one of their sports obligations, provided the student has regularly worked hard in class. But, this will be considered on a case-by-case basis. I will not normally authorize you to reschedule more than one test in the course. I will not authorize student athletes or any other student to reschedule, or extend the deadline for, the global take-home. Under no circumstances will a student that missed a class receive credit under the class participation evaluation component for that class. Written class activities not done in class on the day originally conducted will not be rescheduled or accepted for marking. Homework assignments not submitted personally in class on the due date will not be accepted for marking either.

MISSED CLASS POLICY

If you miss class, please don't ask me for notes—let alone to reteach a class during my office hours or over email. This is because I firmly believe that you learn from constructing and discovering knowledge by yourself and through interaction with your peers, not by reading my notes or listening to me. The learning takes place in class through a carefully designed learning environment that I create based on theoretically grounded and empirically supported teaching and learning strategies. It is unique and cannot be reproduced in my office. So, if you missed a class— for whatever reason—you missed a unique learning experience. No one and nothing can make up for that lost opportunity. If the reason for your absence qualifies you for an extension of an assignment or the reschedule of an evaluation under University policy or current legislation, then you will have the remedy afforded to you by such policy or legislation, but the learning opportunity that you missed is irrecoverable.

**PRIVILEGES: EXTENSIONS, WAIVERS, AND
OTHER AUTHORIZATIONS**

Extensions, waivers, reschedules, rewrites, make-ups, and extra-credit activities are considered privileges, given on a case-by-case basis and as a matter of courtesy. For further clarification, I may or may not grant them or I may grant them to some students and not to others, depending on a number of factors. In general, I will only grant privileges in exceptional circumstances. The following are examples of circumstances that may never be considered exceptional: internet outages, computer or printing problems, compliance with a job supervisor's request to do overtime or an extra shift, or sports commitments. You must plan ahead in order to comply with all the course requirements. This means, among other things, not starting your work the night before the deadline. You must request a privilege in writing. If I grant it, you must keep a copy of the privilege given by me in writing. Privileges not requested in writing and not given in writing are not valid. Occasionally, I may give you the possibility of rewriting a written assignment or some questions from a test. If so, you will forfeit that possibility if you did not attend the class when I returned the original tests or the written assignments. Also, you must rewrite the questions from a test—or hand in the rewritten assignment—on the very next class IN CLASS. Otherwise, you forfeit your privilege to rewrite the questions from a test or to hand in the assignment. Under exceptional, extenuating, and extraordinary circumstances, I may give you as a final grade, a grade that is more than the sum of each evaluation component or I may waive a course requirement other than class participation. I may also give you the possibility of doing activities for extra-credit. If you do not come to class when I distribute the questions or problems for the extra-credit activities, you may not do the extra-credit activities, regardless of the reason for your absence. I may post further rules for extra-credit activities on the course website, which rules may change from time to time. I may also change the attendance policy—or some aspects thereof—in the event classes are interrupted due to a pandemic, or if students have to miss class because of duly documented injury or illness. Please note that medical policies duly adopted by the University may supersede the rules in this course outline, which is not intended to contradict any such University policy.

STUDENTS WITH DISABILITIES

Students with disabilities who would like to discuss classroom and/or exam accommodations should contact me as soon as possible.

ACTION RESEARCH

In order to improve my teaching practice and to enhance student learning, I always conduct classroom action research. For this purpose, I will collect some information about the course and your learning. Sometimes, I will ask you to complete surveys, questionnaires, or other instruments. These are completely voluntary and your responses will be kept strictly confidential. Other times, I will use your classwork as evidence. In all cases, the information will be reported in general terms without specific reference to individual responses or actual names. Completion of the survey, questionnaire, or other instruments implies your consent to participate in the research. If you do not wish to participate, simply let me know before the second class of this course. You will not be penalized for this at all. If you have any questions or concerns about my action research projects, please contact me. Please note that surveys, questionnaires, and other instruments that I will specifically use for action research projects will be anonymous, and they will not be considered for the class participation grade or for any other grade in the course. For further clarification, whether you decide to complete these instruments or not, and your responses to these instruments in the event that you decide to participate, will never be taken into account for grading purposes.

NO RECORDING

No photography, sound-recording, or video recording will be permitted during class without permission. Reproduction of class presentations, activities, course notes, or other similar materials are not permitted without prior written consent. In the case of private use by students with accessibility needs, consent will not be unreasonably withheld.

Sometimes, I will ask you to complete surveys, questionnaires, or other instruments. These are anonymous and voluntary. Your responses will be kept strictly confidential. Other times, I will use your classwork as evidence. In all cases, the information will be reported in general terms without specific reference to individual responses or actual names. Completion of the survey, questionnaire, or other instruments implies your consent to participate in the research. If you do not wish to participate, simply let me know before the second class of this course. You will not be penalized for this at all. If you have any questions or concerns about my action research projects, please contact me. Please note that surveys, questionnaires, and other instruments that I will specifically use for action research projects will be anonymous, and they will not be considered for the class participation grade or for any other grade in the course. For further clarification, whether you decide to complete these instruments or not, and your responses to these instruments in the event that you decide to participate, will never be taken into account for grading purposes.

ACADEMIC DISHONESTY

The University takes a very serious view of such offences as plagiarism, cheating, and impersonation. Penalties for dealing with such offences will be strictly enforced. Please read the Student Code of Conduct (Academic) on plagiarism and other offences against academic honesty. Please note that any self-misrepresentation in order to avoid attendance, meeting of assignment deadlines, writing of tests or examinations and/or completion of assignments, constitutes academic dishonesty. The University website contains a complete policy statement on academic dishonesty and attendance. You are encouraged to read it for further clarification.

TEACHING EVALUATIONS

Please remember to complete the electronic teaching evaluations toward the end of the course. The University considers the evaluation instrumental in assessing teaching. The University will announce the period and instructions for completing the evaluations.

RESEARCH ETHICS

None of the class activities include research involving human beings. However, if you decide that you want to do research involving human beings, such as interviewing or observing, you will need to obtain authorization from the Research Ethics Board BEFORE you start dealing with people. In this case, let me know as soon as possible. I can help you with this process.

FILM COPYRIGHT

If you decide to show a video in class for a class activity or presentation, you must make sure that the University has the copyright to show that video in class, even if it is only an excerpt. This includes videos that you may find online and DVDs that you rent or own. BEFORE showing a video in class, please make sure that you will be able to show it without infringing copyright law. If in doubt, please ask me. You can also check with the library.

INTERNET USE

Many class activities involve doing online searches, reading websites, and posting materials online. You are encouraged to bring to class a laptop, tablet, smartphone, or other electronic device with access to the internet. However, please do not use these devices for any purpose other than to work on the assigned class activity. Any other use is highly disruptive of the learning experience. If you don't have an electronic device with internet access to work with, you may work with a student who has one, use the classroom computer, or go to the computer lab. Please don't feel compelled to buy any device for this class.

TRIGGER WARNINGS

Some materials in this course may be sensitive. Course materials, including lectures, class activities, hypotheticals, scenarios, examples, court cases, and films shown in class, may have mature content, including violent, sexual, and strong language content. Except for newspaper articles and court cases, all class activities are hypothetical and fictitious. Any resemblance to actual persons, institutions, or events is purely coincidental. The views and opinions expressed in the articles assigned for reading in this course are those of the authors and do not necessarily reflect the position of the course professor. Questions, follow-up questions, examples, and comments made within the context of class activities do not purport to state or reflect the opinions or views of the course professor. All such articles, comments, questions, examples, and activities are meant solely to facilitate the discussion and study of Law. They are not meant to advocate or promote any crime or unlawful action. Neither are they meant to advance any ideological perspective. Discretion advised before signing up for this course.

DISCLAIMERS

Trademarks and registered trademarks mentioned in connection with class activities, readings, and assignments are the property of their respective owners. References to trademarks, registered trademarks, commercial products, services by trade name, or real people, living or dead, in the course are for educational purposes only. No claim is made that any such reference constitutes any sponsorship, endorsement, or association of those products, services, or individuals with this course.

Index

For Product Safety Concerns and Information please contact our EU
representative GPSR@taylorandfrancis.com
Taylor & Francis Verlag GmbH, Kaufingerstraße 24, 80331 München, Germany

www.ingramcontent.com/pod-product-compliance
Ingram Content Group UK Ltd.
Pitfield, Milton Keynes, MK11 3LW, UK
UKHW021820240425
457818UK00001B/3